More Praise for *Personal Brilliance:*

"This book is practical and enlightening. *Personal Brilliance* gives readers what they need to know to leverage their natural gifts, and break through the barriers that stop success in its tracks."
> **—Rick Maurer,** author of *Why Don't You Want What I Want?*

"*Personal Brilliance* is one of the most practical, relevant, and powerful books on the market. If being more successful is one of your life goals, you have to read this book."
> **—Roxanne Emmerich,** author of *Thank God It's Monday:*
> *How to Build a Motivating Workplace*

"Coming up with new and better ways to approach your personal life and your career is essential in today's fast-track world. *Personal Brilliance* takes the mystery out of this process, and shows you how to make quantum leaps in your own life."
> **—John Patrick Dolan,** CEO of LawTalk

"Jim Canterucci's dynamic message in his book *Personal Brilliance* can be applied to your personal life, your profession, and even your hobbies. Canterucci really knows his stuff!"
> **—Bob Bailey,** professional speaker and author of
> *Plain Talk About Leadership*

"Reading this book is guaranteed to give you an edge, no matter what arena you're competing in, whether you are on a personal or professional journey. *Personal Brilliance* by Jim Canterucci shows you how to take your natural talents, and use them to achieve success."
> **—Tanya Fratto,** Chief Executive Officer,
> Diamond Innovations, formerly GE Superabrasives

"Jim Canterucci's success formula, while elegantly simple, has profound implications for people in all walks of life. *Personal Brilliance* is right on the mark."
> **—Don Hutson,** CEO of U.S. Learning; and
> author of *Contented Achiever*

"I have seen Canterucci propel people and organizations to achieve their full potential, and he is impressive. The particular power of this book is that his well-designed system shows you how to make personal brilliance a natural part of everything you do, which inevitably results in high levels of personal and professional success."

—Steve Wilson, author of *Good-Hearted Living*

"*Personal Brilliance* by Jim Canterucci is an essential book for anyone who wants to succeed with significance."

—Jack Park, author of *The Official Ohio State Football Encyclopedia* and *Ohio State Football: The Great Tradition*

"Jim Canterucci is the best! And you could be, too. *Personal Brilliance* enables you to access your highest potential at home, at work, and at play."

—Mariah Burton Nelson, athlete, motivational speaker, and author of *The Unburdened Heart: Five Keys to Forgiveness and Freedom* and *We Are All Athletes: Bringing Courage, Confidence, and Peak Performance Into Our Everyday Lives*

"In *Personal Brilliance*, Jim Canterucci takes the hit-or-miss event of innovation, and turns it into a predictable process that everyone can follow. If finding out how to increase your choices, income, and impact are important to you, buy this book today."

—Ken Peters, METTLER TOLEDO, General Manger, North America

"A truly enjoyable book! I found myself immediately excited and enthused to put these principles to good use in every area of my life."

—Lee Glickstein, author of *Be Heard Now!*

"The capacity to think on your feet, approach challenges with a fresh perspective, and open your mind to greater possibilities will propel you to the forefront of any endeavor. *Personal Brilliance* teaches you how to tap into your rich reservoir of talents and abilities, and put them to work."

—Fran Kick, author of *Kick It In & Take the Lead*

Personal Brilliance

Mastering the Everyday Habits
that Create a Lifetime
of Success

Jim Canterucci

Foreword by Nido R. Qubein

⁴AMACOM

American Management Association
New York • Atlanta • Brussels • Chicago • Mexico City • San Francisco
Shanghai • Tokyo • Toronto • Washington, D.C.

Special discounts on bulk quantities of AMACOM books are available to corporations, professional associations, and other organizations. For details, contact Special Sales Department, AMACOM, a division of American Management Association, 1601 Broadway, New York, NY 10019.
Tel.: 212-903-8316.   Fax: 212-903-8083.
Web site: www.amacombooks.org

This publication is designed to provide accurate and authoritative information in regard to the subject matter covered. It is sold with the understanding that the publisher is not engaged in rendering legal, accounting, or other professional service. If legal advice or other expert assistance is required, the services of a competent professional person should be sought.

Library of Congress Cataloging-in-Publication Data

Canterucci, Jim.
    Personal brilliance : mastering the everyday habits that create a lifetime of success / Jim Canterucci.
        p.   cm.
    Includes index.
    ISBN 0-8144-0838-9
    1. Success—Psychological aspects.   I. Title.

BF637.S8C27   2005
158.1—dc22
                                                                    2005005857

Printing Number

10   9   8   7   6   5   4   3   2   1

Contents

Foreword

JIM CANTERUCCI is a genius! He's an innovative thinker, a creative leader, and a very wise coach. Throughout these pages, Jim takes a close look at the four catalysts necessary to spark your brilliance (awareness, curiosity, focus, and initiative) and helps you, the reader, tap into them with thoughtful experience and empathetic understanding. You'll benefit tremendously from reading this book and applying its many practical strategies and proven methods for igniting your personal brilliance.

I've known Jim, both personally and professionally, for a number of years, and I've always admired his capacity to break intellectually solid, yet complex, ideas into comprehensible chunks that anyone could use purposefully to maximize their level of achievement. This book is a good example.

Success results from a sound strategy. Even the greatest ideas are of little value unless they are backed up by a practical and workable plan of action. Jim shares cutting-edge information carefully framed with effective exercises, a Personal Brilliance Assessment, and tons of insights—all adding up to a plan you can start now to enhance your life and be more, do more, and give more.

What I appreciate most about this book and about Jim's work is the evident balance between knowledge and skill, between experience and wisdom, between success and significance. He honestly and openly acknowledges that we must differentiate ourselves if we are to survive and thrive in our increasingly competitive world. Whether you are a CEO or a stay-at-home parent, you'll benefit immensely from this book's generous inclusion of tested ideas, fun exercises, and on-target illustrations. He refers to many timely examples of innovation throughout the history of humankind, but he quickly admits that it is the process of innovation—the way we think and live—that truly ensures the greatest benefit in our lives.

Enjoy this book. Read it with an appetite for learning. Apply it with a commitment for excellence. Live it for a guarantee of cherishing the benefits of attaining the habits that unleash your personal brilliance!

Nido R. Qubein
Chairman, Great Harvest Bread Company;
President, High Point University

Acknowledgments

A BOOK truly is a slice of the author's life. I would like to use this space to acknowledge only some who have helped shape this life so far. Murray Mika and Dennis Heebink are owed a great deal for caring enough to help shape a youngster in business. My clients are a big part of this book. They have taught me so much while allowing me the honor of teaching them. My 7 Figures Circle coaching participants are critical in forcing me to articulate my ideas in a practical, usable way. My fellow professionals in the National Speakers Association, and particularly NSA Ohio, are instrumental in my life.

Thank you, Lillian Zarzar, for telling your audiences to buy this book before I thought of writing it. Without the assistance of my friend, colleague, and writing coach, Tonianne Robino, this book would not be possible.

I am grateful to all of the wonderful people at AMACOM and to my literary agent Jeff Herman for walking me through this experience. Additionally, there are a number of friends and colleagues throughout the world who have embraced this work and are sharing it with as many people as possible. Thank you.

Words can't describe the contribution of Holly Canterucci

to this work and to my life. She embodies the most complete definition of partner.

Finally, I would like to thank you, the reader, for embarking on this journey. I look forward to a long, rewarding relationship.

Introduction

WHETHER WE LIKE IT OR NOT, the world today is a more competitive place. This is true for corporate titans competing for market dominance, for Betty competing with Jeff to lead the new department, and also for moms and dads competing with Madison Avenue marketers for the attention of their children. This book is designed to help you enhance the inner strengths that will allow you to differentiate yourself in your world.

The information age has resulted in volumes of data on most any subject. This has caused an imbalance, and finer degrees of specialization have emerged. Ironically, rather than making our lives easier and more efficient, the wealth of specialized information has had the opposite effect. We seem to have less time and resources to accomplish all that's necessary, and we need to be more well-rounded to accomplish what we set out to do. It's no wonder that stress levels and depression are at an all-time high.

This book is about hope and possibility. You already have the tools. No matter the current location on your path of development and growth, *Personal Brilliance* will provide a context for negotiating life at your personal best. This book is about bringing an innovative solution and value to any situation. Although there are stories of some of the most brilliant characters of our time, we're focusing on brilliance in every-day activities, like having a positive impact on a teenager, solving the marketing problem at work, or determining how to best raise money for your charitable cause. *Personal Brilliance* will support you in many ways. The benefits apply whether you are a stay-at-home parent, a professional, a corporate manager, a student, an entrepreneur, or a front-line worker.

The four catalysts to Personal Brilliance are awareness, curiosity, focus, and initiative. These are natural gifts that can be enhanced with practice and exercise. These catalysts have been identified as the factors that contribute to personal brilliance, based on years of consulting and personal coaching. The ideas have been tested with scores of clients. Each catalyst is represented in a separate section of the book. Each section lays the foundation for the catalyst, identifies some barriers that may exist and how they can be overcome, and provides a new set of strategies to leverage your strengths so you can amplify, heighten, expand, and intensify your innate abilities.

To help you determine how to best absorb the material, you can connect to an online assessment of your current Personal Brilliance Quotient and receive tips on how best to work with *Personal Brilliance*.

This isn't a quick fix. Study and practice is necessary to shift your habits to consistently approach life in an innovative way. However, in many areas you will see results quickly. Please read this book with a highlighter and a *Personal Brilliance Notebook* (explained in Chapter 2) to capture the ideas that have the greatest impact for you.

There also are many exercises to choose from. I suggest that you try them all at least once, and repeat the ones that bring you the greatest results. By taking this approach, you will be embarking on an innovative journey and be able to identify your personal milestones as you travel this course.

If you are part of a team seeking growth, provide a copy of this book for everyone on your team, including your clients. Families can benefit from working on this material together as well. The synchronicity and momentum created by implementing the awareness, curiosity, focus, and initiative strategies as a group will ensure that you meet your targets much sooner than anticipated.

Let's get started. Use *Personal Brilliance* to bring increased innovation and value to your future.

Enjoy the journey!

YOU ALREADY HAVE WHAT YOU NEED

CHAPTER 1

Live Your Picture of
SUCCESS

Success in life is founded upon ATTENTION to the small things rather that to the large things; to the every day things nearest to us rather than to the things that are remote and uncommon.

BOOKER T. WASHINGTON
AFRICAN-AMERICAN LEADER AND EDUCATOR

HOW do you define success? Is success material wealth: a big house, a fancy car, a great job, financial security? Is success about family and social relationships: a happy home life, stable children, wonderful friends? Is success related to health: staying fit, being active, living a long life? Is success about spiritual growth and development: a fulfilling belief system, religious affiliation, communing with a higher power? What does success mean to you?

For me, the most useful definition of success incorporates all of these areas of life and others as well. A great way to measure success is to identify the number of choices available at any given moment. If we look at two men, who are exactly the same in every observable way—with the same job, same financial status, and same family life—one may be more successful than the other. For example, if one man loves his job and the other is holding onto his job because he has to, which one is more successful?

If you're in the job market and have two or three options, or when house hunting you can choose among four neighborhoods, you are more successful than if you had no job offers or if three of the four neighborhoods were out of reach. The number of choices available to you is a reflection of your previous work and track record. The number of choices available is a fair measure of success.

In every situation there is more than one option. Can you see all of the choices? Can you see the nuances of the choices? There are very few scenarios in which the answers are simply black or white. Success—and the opportunities that create it—lies in the gray area. And that's where your personal brilliance comes into play. Personal brilliance will help you succeed no matter what success means to you.

Developing Your Personal Brilliance

One's philosophy is not best expressed in words; it is expressed in the choices that one makes. In the long run, we shape our lives and we shape ourselves. The process never ends until we die. And, the choices we make are ultimately our own responsibility.

ELEANOR ROOSEVELT
U.S. FIRST LADY AND COLUMNIST

This book is not about creativity, although creativity is a prerequisite for personal brilliance. Creativity is the process of generating something new. Everyone possesses an innate capacity for creativity, which is a skill. It involves intuition and the right side of the brain. There are a number of tools to enhance creativity, and investing time developing your creative capacity is time well spent.

This book is about personal innovation. While creativity

is the process of generating something new, *innovation* is the practical application of creativity into something that has an impact.

Developing your personal brilliance is about expanding your natural abilities, allowing you to be consistently innovative, and creating a lifetime of success.

Although we're talking about innovation on a personal, everyday level, we'll discuss some famous innovations from our history. The question comes up, do we really need innovation? Did we need the printing press? Did we need television? Did we need Velcro? Did we need the automobile? How about the cell phone?

We could have survived without these innovations, but it's obvious that they've had a deep impact on our lives. As a species, we have the capacity for brilliance. It's in our nature. All of us are capable of brilliance at these lofty levels as well as in our day-to-day lives. We don't necessarily need the resulting innovation, but I think we do need the process of innovation, applying our personal brilliance, to help fulfill our nature.

Will we all invent something like the light bulb or air conditioning? Maybe not. You can take this as far as you want to. The most important thing is to use these concepts every day. Personal brilliance is not just for the scientist in a laboratory or for the high-tech guru or for the CEO. Personal brilliance is also for the entry-level employee, the team leader working with six team members, the manager of an accounting group, the production line worker, or the project manager. These concepts can also be applied in our personal lives as parents, spouses, or family members.

For instance, one busy mother got tired of juggling work demands with last-minute requests from her kids. She decided to train her children in time management by having a planning-time session on Sunday evenings, at which time all her children had to tell her what activities they had planned for the coming week. Then, if they asked to do something and it wasn't on the weekly schedule, the answer would be "no" unless it was a true "life or death" emergency. Soon, when the children's "I forgot to tell you" resulted in mom saying, "Next week you'll remember to plan early" instead of hectic last minute changes, sanity returned to her schedule: personal brilliance, in a real life situation.

Habits Make It Easy

Being yourself is not remaining what you were, or being satisfied with what you are. It is the point of departure.

SYDNEY J. HARRIS
BRITISH AUTHOR

A habit is something that you do so often and so regularly that it becomes automatic. This is a behavior that you can easily repeat. When I work with people I try to determine their habits because most of our behaviors are based on our habits.

Our habits are directly related to our comfort and well-being. The process of adapting to our environment is what creates a habit. With habits we don't have to constantly experiment or deal with unknown risks.

There are habits built into the most seemingly chaotic environments. I travel extensively and constantly encounter security checks, delayed luggage, and canceled flights. The only way I can navigate this world somewhat calmly is with many small habits, such as putting my tickets and passport in the same briefcase compartment every time, packing my carry-on so that I can survive 24 hours without the rest of my luggage, and carrying a backup computer disk that contains my presentation materials in the event the boxes I ship don't make it. With all the variables, the more steps and processes that are automatic, the more flexibility and capacity we have to deal with whatever crops up.

Our habits help define us. The way we adapt to our environment and how we typically behave say a lot about who we are as human beings. What do we know about someone with the habit of not eating meat? What about someone with the habit of smoking cigarettes? How about the person with the habit of running five miles each day?

Habits are extremely difficult to change because they are tied to our identities. Notice that I haven't said anything about "breaking a habit." I avoid that terminology because a habit is dependent on repetition. Therefore, if we replace the activity that is the former habit—such as lighting a cigarette after dinner—with some other activity—such as taking a walk or chewing a stick of gum—the repetition ceases and the coding of the smoking habit is reduced dramatically.

The key to succeeding in replacing old habits with new ones is ensuring that the new behaviors are more appealing, effective, and beneficial than their predecessors. The exercises in the upcoming chapters are designed to serve as replacement activities: filling up the available space with new actions, exercising different areas of your capabilities, and possibly replacing some old habits that may not be serving your definition of success.

In effect, replacing less effective habits with more effective ones and creating new habits that foster greater success and well-being are the most expedient ways to increase and expand your personal brilliance.

Imagination plus innovation equals realization.

DENIS WAITLEY
AUTHOR AND "PEAK PERFORMANCE" EXPERT

Simply by investing in a copy of *Personal Brilliance* you have proven that you likely are more innovative than many in our population. I also think that you are probably much more innovative than you think you are. When I surveyed hundreds of people, a cross-section of people with varying backgrounds, I learned something very surprising. Some of the most personally brilliant people I know don't think they're innovative! It's easier to observe innovation in someone else than in yourself.

This book is not designed to fix you. You're not broken. But, we can all go deeper in improving the habits that lead to personal brilliance. Chances are, you're already being innovative in one or more areas of your life, whether it's the novel approach you take to get your kids to do their homework, or the cutting-edge marketing plan you've devised for your business. However, no matter how innovative you are right now, there's always room for improvement. By following the program in this book, you're on the way to making personal brilliance the rule, rather than the exception.

CHAPTER 2

The Power of FOUR

Your Natural Abilities Add Up to Personal Brilliance

It's a funny thing about life; if you refuse to accept anything but the best, you very often get it.

W. SOMERSET MAUGHAM
BRITISH NOVELIST AND PLAYWRIGHT

THERE ARE FOUR catalysts to enhance your personal brilliance that will be the cornerstones for this journey. They are Awareness, Curiosity, Focus, and Initiative. All four catalysts are innate abilities, possessed by each of us.

Awareness involves self-awareness first (the hardest part), then being conscious of your environment, and being cognizant of the actual problem at hand. As you generate an awareness of a particular issue or challenge, it has to really become a part of you. In conversations you have with others, you bring up this issue or challenge (verbally or nonverbally). The issue is just below the surface when you're reading a book or article. You think about it subconsciously in everything you do.

Each conversation and interaction provides you with more to think about. You develop a *curiosity* as you think, looking in many different arenas for insights. You pay attention to all aspects of your life with this filter, seeking to solve the problem. You look at the obvious things, but your curiosity helps you go deeper.

While going about your business on a day-to-day basis you are extremely *focused* on the problem. I'm not talking about a laser beam focus. I'm referring to a 360-degree focus, more like a spotlight whose beam widens out. You don't want to limit yourself. Your focused attention should allow you to be open to any possible solutions that are floating out there.

You're going to come up with many ideas and options through your awareness, curiosity, and focus. The fourth catalyst, *initiative*, is necessary both to allow this process to work and also to ultimately implement the solution. It's about taking action. This book is about innovation in all of your endeavors and building the habits that will enhance your personal brilliance resulting in frequent innovations.

Each of the four catalysts—awareness, curiosity, focus, and initiative—is invaluable, but when you combine their forces, you will literally astound yourself. However, coming up with a new idea or solving a problem hardly ever occurs by using these catalysts in a linear order, such as first doing this, and then doing that. While it's possible to be intrigued with an idea, then increasing your awareness, exercising your curiosity about the topic, getting focused, and finally taking action, it's more likely that two or more of these catalysts will be engaged at the same time. You'll find that these catalysts work together seamlessly.

Turning all four of these innate abilities into daily habits and using them together makes the wheel of personal innovation spin! By harnessing the power of each of these habits, your level of personal success and fulfillment will soar. Chances are that one or two of your personal brilliance catalysts are more developed than others. That's terrific! Now it's time to bring the other abilities up to speed. Remember that all four are of equal importance and all four must be made daily habits to create the best possible outcomes. If you allow one of these habits to dominate the others, there's a good chance you'll miss an important piece of the big picture.

Making the Best Use of This Book

The Personal Brilliance Quotient

> *With regard to excellence, it is not enough to know,*
> *but we must try to have and use it.*
>
> ARISTOTLE
> *NICHOMACHEAN ETHICS*

The first step in making personal brilliance a habit is to take a look at how you currently respond to challenges, solve problems, and come up with new or improved ideas or methods. The Personal Brilliance Quotient Assessment will help you determine how well you are using your natural gifts of awareness, curiosity, focus, and initiative. Based on your results, you can decide where to place the most attention. For example, if you score very high in curiosity, but only average in focus, you may want to go directly to the Focus section of the book (Chapters 11 to 14) and come back to the Curiosity section later. The sections are designed so that you can proceed in any order. To access the Personal Brilliance Quotient Assessment, go to the Web site at *www.MyPersonalBrilliance .com.*

The assessment only takes about ten minutes to complete and most of the people who have completed it said it was easy and even fun to do. You can certainly derive significant benefits from reading this book and doing the exercises and practices *without* taking the assessment, but I think you'll find that increasing your self-awareness before you proceed to the next chapters will benefit you even more.

Personal Brilliance Notebook

A rock pile ceases to be a rock pile the moment a single man contemplates it, bearing within him the image of a cathedral.

ANTOINE DE SAINT-EXUPÉRY
FRENCH AUTHOR AND AVIATOR

There are many exercises in this book and I suggest recording information in a *Personal Brilliance Notebook* as you go through the material. Use a notebook you can conveniently carry with you. Rather than writing your insights and ideas on scraps of paper, napkins, or in the margins of books, collect all of your thoughts in one central location. You may want to choose a small notebook that fits in your briefcase or handbag, a standard size spiral notebook, or even a thin three-ring binder.

For options, visit *www.MyPersonalBrilliance.com.* Many of my clients like to use three-ring binders or notebooks with pockets, so that they can also place articles of interest and newspaper clippings inside. Any notebook will work, but choosing a color and style that appeals to you can make the process more fun.

In your *Personal Brilliance Notebook*, write down your day-to-day observations and insights. As you begin to open new pathways in your brain, ideas will begin to flow—sometimes at inconvenient times. Your *Personal Brilliance Notebook* can serve as a repository for these great ideas. You can review these ideas any time and begin to plan how you will implement the best of them.

SECTION II

AWARENESS

CHAPTER 3

The Power of AWARENESS

> We are all on a spiral path. No growth takes place in a straight line. There will be setbacks along the way. . . . There will be shadows, but they will be balanced by patches of light and fountains of joy as we grow and progress. Awareness of the pattern is all you need to sustain you along the way.
>
> KRISTIN ZAMBUCKA
> AUTHOR

YOUR GIFT of awareness is an integral part of personal brilliance. When you use your awareness optimally, you are present, mindful, alert, and grounded. You're positioned to see the highest number of options and you're able to grasp the cause and effect relationships that are creating your current opportunity or dilemma.

AWARENESS
CURIOSITY
FOCUS
INITIATIVE

Becoming more aware means becoming conscious of more: more facts, more objects, more opinions, more sensations, more perceptions, more feelings, more thoughts. We strive to see more pieces of any given puzzle. Being aware of more is the first step in beginning to see connections between ideas. Seeing the bigger picture and making more connections leads to a brilliant result. Awareness is the equivalent of being able to open your eyes to begin the process of seeing.

If a chess master can see ten moves ahead and an opponent can see only three moves ahead we can easily predict the winner. A businessperson considering a new deal is much more effective when her power of awareness allows a view of the many variables inherent in the deal. A father's awareness can make all the difference in preventing or addressing his teenager's drug experimentation.

Enhancing Awareness and Concentration

There can only be one state of mind as you approach any profound test; total concentration, a spirit of togetherness, and strength.

PAT RILEY
MOTIVATIONAL SPEAKER AND FORMER NBA COACH

In attempting to understand and develop awareness we will briefly explore attention—the ability to observe and sense directly. We will also explore consciousness—the ability to observe our own thinking. Awareness incorporates attention and consciousness, as well as the capacity to observe how we feel.

Our exploration of awareness looks at both self-awareness—what's happening inside of us—as well as external awareness—what's happening outside of us in the environment in which we exist. People who do not know their strengths and weaknesses and who don't listen to their intuition are certainly at a disadvantage. The combination is important here. Without both internal and external awareness, it isn't possible to reap the overall benefits of awareness.

It is very common in any business arena to overhear conversations among disgruntled employees who are complaining about their situations. Perhaps they're bored or they've been passed over for some opportunity. Often the focus of the conversation is externally focused: "Can you believe how unfair the boss is?" With a small dose of self-awareness, the employees may admit that their skills are stale.

Without self-awareness, important evidence indicating a need for self-development can be ignored. For example, you may find that the boss frequently misunderstands you. A short course on communication style may solve the problem. On the other hand, a reduced level of self-awareness also has an impact, causing us to ignore opportunities that arise. In effect, we aren't prepared to see that we are qualified and prepared for an opportunity. Awareness is a powerful, yet simple, way to get in touch with our own wisdom.

In regard to external awareness, there are many examples of company leaders ignoring mountains of evidence that their ways of approaching the business were no longer appropriate until it was too late to avoid serious trouble. How many "dot bombs" can you name? In any failed project it is easy to see what the leader missed in the process. There are easy-to-identify signposts that were missed. Hindsight is twenty-twenty, so how do we avoid missing these signposts when they crop up in our own lives? The answer is to increase our awareness.

Awareness Is the Key to Achieving Goals

What is a demanding pleasure that demands the use of one's mind! Not in the sense of problem solving, but in the sense of exercising discrimination, judgment, awareness.

AYN RAND
WRITER AND PHILOSOPHER

The beginning of any strategy—whether it's in the corporate world, the public sector, the arts, or our personal life—is an analysis of the environment. That analysis is based on the awareness of where we are, who we are, what we are, and who we will be interacting with in the particular environment. The key to any positive change is an acute awareness of the problem. Only after we see the problem can we begin to solve it.

The opposite of awareness is a robotic mechanical journey through life. The faster the rate of change in our environment, the more dangerous it is to operate with a dampened awareness. Naturally, in a state of dampened awareness we are dependent upon approaches that may no longer apply in the new, changing circumstances or situation.

We have evolved to a modern information economy. It is clear that a higher level of education, more knowledge, and different skills are needed today than in the past. However, what may not be so clear is that to be successful in this economy there is a need for a much higher level of self in the form of taking greater responsibility, having a full appreciation of the atmosphere at any given point, and making informed choices. To take full advantage of the opportunities presented, you need to bring a higher level of awareness to your tasks and interactions.

In generations past, our future was preordained. We simply carried on the family skill. If you were a man, and your father was a blacksmith, you became a blacksmith. If you were a woman, you married into another family and supported the skill or profession of your husband and his family. In effect, people were born into a place where custom or those who came before made decisions for them. In my parents' generation, it was not the normal practice to move away from the town in which you grew up. My mother literally moved across the driveway upon marriage. I grew up next door to my grandparents.

Today we are faced with an abundance of choices. Where to live, what schools to attend, what career to choose, whether and when to marry, who your marriage partner will be, whether or not to have children, and how many children to have are all choices that are relatively new ones in our society. In simpler times we could lean on custom and tradition for guidance. Now that the choices are ours, this freedom requires us to use our own resources more than ever before. This increased self-reliance on our own ability to think and act requires a more active awareness.

When faced with more choices, clear vision is always preferable to foggy notions. The more aware we are of the details that may affect our lives, the greater chance that we will make wise choices and act effectively.

I like to think of awareness as a light that is sweeping over the environment, much like the sun shines on the ground as clouds move away. The sun is always shining. Whether or not the sun illuminates the situation is a function of the clouds blocking the light. We can control the "movement" of the clouds in our lives by controlling our awareness. Bring light to your environment. Our awareness operates on a continuum from intense awareness—in which every nuance of the situation is available to us—to the opposite extreme in which we are not aware at all, as in a situation where we are in a deep sleep or coma. As long as we are physically conscious, we have a choice regarding how aware we are in our life at any given point. Living at either end of the awareness spectrum is not realistic or valuable. It is a matter of determining the degree of awareness appropriate for the issue in front of us. This really is a matter of control.

Consider the phenomenon of a minor injury, such as an ankle sprain. Where your awareness is focused determines the level of pain, within limits of course. For example, if you are lying quietly with your foot elevated and you begin thinking of your commute to work tomorrow you may experience pain at level 3 on a 1-to-5 scale, with 5 being extreme pain. If, however, you begin reading a novel or watching TV, your awareness will shift to imaginary places and activities far removed from the use of your ankle, and the pain level may be reduced to a 1 or even a 0.

Tuning In and Tuning Out

*Only one thing has to change for us to know happiness in
our lives: where we focus our attention.*

GREG ANDERSON
THE 22 NON-NEGOTIABLE LAWS OF WELLNESS

To be most effective you need to learn what you should pay
attention to and what to leave on automatic. Context determines the appropriate level of awareness. There are simple
physical tasks you can perform with very little awareness or
attention. After some practice you can drive a car while listening to music or talking with a passenger. But have you noticed
that when a traffic problem presents itself your awareness
abruptly shifts from the music or the conversation to the road
in front of you? The siren from a passing emergency vehicle
can quickly (in micro-seconds) shift your awareness from
thinking about the grocery list to where you will pull over. If
you're in a mindful state you can recognize when it is wise to
apply greater awareness to one aspect of your environment
over another. As we'll discuss in the Focus section, there is a
difference between exclusive focus and appropriate focus.

Another way to think about the context or appropriateness
of your awareness is to compare the four-year-old riding a
bike two days after removing the training wheels with the
twelve-year-old who uses her bike as her primary mode of
transportation. The twelve-year-old is much more adept at
riding her bike than the four-year-old, but the younger, less
experienced rider is much more aware of the mechanical
steps of riding her bike. We feel the twelve-year-old is safer,
even though she isn't paying attention to the actual bike riding. We feel more comfortable mainly because we know she
has a greater awareness of her total environment—attending
to curbs, cars, passing friends, and so on—while mechanically

handling the task of maneuvering the bike. In any desire for mastery we seek the state where we can be mechanical when appropriate, allowing a greater awareness of outside factors that may affect performance.

All of us operate with more awareness in some areas than in others, based on our preferences, skills, and experiences. Some people are very aware of work-related issues but apply very little awareness in the political arena. Some people are very aware of health-related issues but lack awareness in the area of personal relationships. This fact provides a great deal of hope for improvement. You don't need to learn how to develop awareness from scratch. Rather you can apply what you know in one area of your life to other areas of your life.

Living with awareness is a state of being mentally active rather than passive. It takes effort and commitment. You should seek to be aware of all that has an impact on your life. You must confront reality whether it's pleasant or not. Within the context you choose, being aware means actively seeking understanding. The pursuit of awareness requires courage, because reality is not always to our liking. To live with awareness requires us to not only be aware but also to act accordingly. Unfortunately, you can't always have a successful result, but the active pursuit of our goals with a honed awareness increases the odds of success.

The Power of Presence

Presence is more than just being there.

MALCOLM S. FORBES
THE FURTHER SAYINGS OF CHAIRMAN MALCOLM

Awareness is slowing down. It is often said that as we get older time flies by more quickly. Perhaps this is because as we age and mature and our lives become more complicated, we suppress our natural awareness in order to cope. Consequently, we miss a great deal. We live outside the present moment much more than we did as a child. By suspending judgment and simply paying attention to what's happening in the present moment, we're in touch with "what is." Otherwise, the hours, days, months, and years go by unnoticed and unappreciated.

To be aware, you have to make a habit of pausing to let the present moment sink in and be conscious of all its aspects. If you're focused on the past or worried about the future, it's not possible to be in control of your life and of the effect you have on the world.

If you are present in what you are doing, you are able to receive the information that you need. Now is the only time you have to live, grow, and feel. Being present gives you the ability to be open to new opportunities and choices resulting in a life of greater enjoyment. To live in a present awareness in which you can appreciate the wonderful experiences right now, it's necessary to set aside worries about the future and past baggage.

Self-awareness includes being conscious of your physical processes as well as your mental processes and emotions. If you're willing to be totally present without denial, the result is a more vivid awareness. Innovative individuals value their inner signals and therefore tend to be more autonomous.

To become more self-aware, start noticing your thoughts—where they are and how they affect your emotions and actions. When they are not in the present, you miss your life's magnificence and opportunities as well as subtle signals of trouble. Don't get caught up in your thoughts, including opinions about yourself. They are not "reality." They are perceptions. Believe it or not, innovators live in reality.

Self-awareness is not narcissism. That is not helpful. Instead, you need to be aware of yourself as an additional contributor to the process of growth, treating yourself just as you would treat others brought together to reach a goal or solve a problem.

Being Aware of Others

The whole idea of compassion is based on a keen awareness of the interdependence of all these living beings, which are all part of one another, and all involved in one another.

THOMAS MERTON
RELIGIOUS WRITER AND POET

A focal point in my work with those who are guiding the implementation of large changes in business organizations is enhancing the skills that lead them to being more empathetic with those absorbing the change. Active listening is a key skill set. Awareness is an underlying foundation in active listening. Bringing acute awareness to an interaction with another human being is the way to show respect for that individual. Communication breaks down when awareness breaks down. The probability for success in our interactions can be increased a great deal if the other individual feels he or she is understood.

Being aware is critical to basic interactions between humans. The next time you are out for a casual lunch or dinner, notice your interactions with the server. Now, think about a similar meal, but one in which what is happening with your guests is very important to you, such as negotiating a business deal. How is your awareness of the server different? Is there a parallel to your awareness of the server and the quality of service you receive?

My firm, Transition Management Advisors, focuses on the

leadership of organizational change. Empathy, a product of awareness, is a key to successful change leadership. Reconciling change is a process. I often counsel executive clients to maintain a log of their process for personally dealing with a major change so they can help their staff in the coming weeks as they travel the same path.

I am fortunate to have a vibrant, strong, and beautiful relationship with my wife. I believe we both applied *all* the principles discussed in this book—awareness, curiosity, focus, and initiative—prior to our wedding to make sure we were right for each other, and we continue to use these catalysts many years later. But awareness is also important for making the marriage work on a day-to-day basis. I'm not a marriage or personal relationship counselor but I can tell you how these principles work for us.

First of all, it's critical that we are self-aware. Knowing what my triggers are, what gets me fired up, and what my common reactions to situations are helps provide a context for the relationship. Coupled with this self-awareness, an external awareness of my partner is the other side of the coin.

I'm talking about consistently being aware of your partner—literally hearing, seeing, and feeling. Some examples of this awareness are: picking up on the feelings of your partner in different situations, noticing subtle differences in the feelings during interactions, watching how your partner perceives others compared to how you perceive them, and knowing the signals for approval or disapproval. This is just a short list. Being aware starts the process for making relationship choices that deepen the bond rather than strain it.

Awareness is an important catalyst. In the remaining chapters of this section we'll examine the natural capacity we have for awareness, share examples of awareness paying off, identify some barriers to awareness and ways to overcome them, and explore practices to amplify your awareness.

CHAPTER 4

You're Designed for Optimal
AWARENESS

The greatest obstacle to discovery is not
ignorance—it is the illusion of knowledge.
DANIEL BOORSTIN
"THE 6 O'CLOCK SCHOLAR," THE WASHINGTON POST

YOUR MIND and body have built-in sensors that give you an incredible capacity to take in information, sort and process it, and either store or delete it. As an infant, you were constantly paying attention to all of the sights and sounds around you. Wide-eyed with wonder, your eyes traveled around the nursery soaking up every detail from the bright pink nose on your little brown bunny to the stars and stripes on your crib. You didn't want to miss a thing.

> AWARENESS
> CURIOSITY
> FOCUS
> INITIATIVE

The awareness level that infants achieve effortlessly is your natural capacity. However, for many people awareness is reduced as age increases. This may be understandable when you're nearing the end of your life, but to allow it to happen when you're in your prime seems foolish. If you want to live your life to its fullest, practice bringing your physical and mental awareness back up to speed.

Awareness is evidence of being alive. Information reaches your consciousness through the filter of awareness. You can control the extent of your awareness. Therefore, you control what you let inside your consciousness.

Awareness requires a great deal of your available attention. Attention involves working with or manipulating your consciousness. From all the varied stimuli available to us, we choose what stimuli to bring into our awareness. Because awareness is so complex, we tend to minimize it during periods of great stress, which unfortunately is when we need it most. This can explain why eyewitness accounts of a stressful event, such as an armed robbery, are so unreliable. We also shut down awareness when we sleep. However, dreams we can recall when we wake up represent an awareness of our mental activity during sleep. The phrase "Wake Up" is frequently used to jar someone's awareness. You can learn to be aware more frequently and consistently.

Another example of the difference between consciousness and awareness is a patient under anesthesia. Under anesthesia you are not aware. You likely are conscious, however, as it can be demonstrated that you are able to understand and react appropriately to spoken directions when under anesthesia. You are conscious of these directions while not being aware of your consciousness.

Brain researcher Ken Giuffré, M.D., uses the analogy of a head of broccoli to explain how our brains function:

If there were twenty individual pieces of broccoli tied together to form a bunch, the conscious state—what we are aware of, what we are thinking, and the resources we have access to—may comprise for example, three or four of the twenty. Thus, if we are used to performing a certain repertoire of tasks, such as an accountant working with figures all day, our state of mind during that time will become more and more efficient, using the smallest brain area possible to get the work done. Our conscious state will tend to represent a narrower representation of our whole brain, using two or three pieces of broccoli and will tend to ignore the other seventeen or eighteen.

Dr. Giuffré goes on to say:

As we begin to challenge ourselves with new tasks outside our area of expertise, and incorporate knowledge outside our zone of familiarity, we force our brain to expand outside our familiar two to three pieces of broccoli. This begins to build connection pathways from familiar, well-used areas of the brain to less used, but available areas of our brain. As we become more "broad minded" we create new accessory neural pathways from familiar to unfamiliar subsets. Our conscious state is able to have access to more brain resources and we become more adaptive and creative in our primary area of pursuit.

The innovative person uses a number of stalks in the head of broccoli, not just the minimum requirement. This increased brain usage represents increased awareness allowing a much richer experience.

Awareness Is Not Based on Intelligence

Only the curious will learn and only the resolute overcome the obstacles to learning. The quest quotient has always excited me more than the intelligence quotient.

EUGENE S. WILSON
EDUCATOR

Is a certain level of intelligence necessary for optimal awareness? Intellectual ability is not relevant. When we use the phrase "personal brilliance" we think of intelligent people, but it's clear that there are many kinds of intelligence. All of us have the ability to increase awareness in our own way. Perhaps the environment and the scenarios we face are different according to our intelligence level, but the process is the same. There are many examples of individuals considered to be mentally handicapped who have very high levels of awareness and who can provide significant input to a situation. They may do this in a simpler, less sophisticated way, but the key is picking up what might otherwise be missed.

In fact, we can be aware of something and observe it without knowing about it. When consciousness of an event occurs in the brain and where it occurs is in debate among neuroscientists and isn't that important to our discussion. When we discuss awareness, we simply want to notice the thunder and lightning during a storm. We don't necessarily need to understand why the light and sound reach us separately. Curiosity will kick in and help us ask the question that will lead to the answer regarding the difference in the speed of sound and light, which we may apply somewhere else. It starts with observation—awareness. For example, it's possible to be stalked by a killer during a thunderstorm, to be shot at by the stalker, and to be less aware of the thunder and lightning (or barely even notice it) because our life is in danger.

Reason Requires a Balanced Perspective

Most of our so-called reasoning consists in finding arguments for going on believing as we already do.

JAMES HARVEY ROBINSON
THE MIND IN THE MAKING

Life is a constantly evolving puzzle. When faced with a puzzle that may take the form of "How do I make the sale," or "How do I assist my child to select the correct school," or "How do I get out of debt," we humans are armed with the ability to reason. As a species, we have evolved our ability to reason, taking awareness to a level that allows integration of many distinct pieces of data to help solve the puzzle. This is where I sometimes begin losing people. Some feel they just aren't good problem solvers because they tend to make decisions based on feelings or their "gut."

My advice is to not think of reason as separate from the emotion-based response. Reason isn't only a mental process. We've talked about context as it relates to awareness. Your belief system needs to be considered in the process of problem solving. Being aware of these beliefs is the first step. You need to ask yourself why you believe what you do. Is ignorance the basis for your viewpoints, or is fear? Reason involves the integration of experiences in a noncontradictory way. The more you can be open and aware of each experience, the greater the likelihood of solid reasoning.

What contradictions are there in your thinking? Most people are unaware that their thoughts, actions, and values are full of contradictions. Do you preach telling the truth to your children and then tell a little white lie here and there? Are you politically correct in your language relating to the opposite sex but stuck with the stereotypes you learned from a previous generation? Did you complain about your old boss only to find yourself doing the same things he did? What is your assumed truth? Check your assumptions.

Proper reasoning involves both positives and negatives. Adequate awareness may uncover glitches in your way of thinking. You need to be able to acknowledge these gaps and adjust accordingly.

Responsibility Motivates Awareness

The price of greatness is responsibility.

WINSTON CHURCHILL
BRITISH STATESMAN AND PRIME MINISTER

"It's not my job." Responsibility is the motivation for aware-ness. In my executive advisory role, I have met with many leaders who are baffled by example after example of their em-ployees' lack of awareness. The common complaint is, "How did they miss the obvious writing on the wall?" The answer lies in a lack of empowerment or responsibility on the part of the employees. If they don't feel responsible, don't have some sort of stake in the process, they will literally not "see" what they need to see to be effective. When there is little responsi-bility or accountability, there is little motivation to raise awareness.

Take responsibility! Take ownership. In a work setting the best employees treat the business as if they are owners, whether they are or not. Take responsibility for the words you use. Listen for how your words may affect the people hearing them. Be conscious of your words and their impact.

Most people are only aware of what they have learned to be aware of and therefore miss a great deal. In my presenta-tions, I ask the audience to jot down the number four as it appears on their watches (without looking at the watch). We look at our watches countless times during the day but many audience members can't successfully complete the exercise. My watch shows the number four as IIII, a doctored Roman numeral. If we miss something as mundane as what the face of our watch looks like, what else are we missing?

The Role of Consciousness

*When you are inspired by some great purpose, some
extraordinary project, all your thoughts break their bonds,
your mind transcends limitations, your consciousness
expands in every direction, and you find yourself in a new,
great, and wonderful world. Dormant forces, faculties, and
talents become alive, and you discover yourself to be a
greater person by far than you ever dreamed yourself to be.*

PATANJALI
INDIAN PHILOSOPHER

Consciousness is used to monitor the environment for us,
bringing stimuli from the environment to our attention and
awareness. This process can be seen when we are quietly
reading inside our home on a windy day. Our focus is on the
reading and our awareness includes the book, possibly the
comfortable feeling of being inside, and the sound of the wind
outside. We are aware of many things but our primary focus
is on the story we are reading and the overall experience.
However, our consciousness shifts our attention and awareness very quickly when we suddenly hear a loud scraping
sound on the side of the house. The story we are reading
quickly leaves our awareness and is replaced with the possibility of damage from a fallen tree. Our hearing becomes more
focused; we jump up to look outside with all antennae tuned
to finding out what happened and to determine whether we
or our house are in danger.

Consciousness is a process of observation. What are you
aware of? You can work on this. You can develop your process
of awareness and your filter of consciousness. Law enforce-
ment officials are trained to walk into a room and with a quick
glance accurately report the smallest details of the contents in
the room. This comes with training. Awareness is based on

our training and interests. When driving with an off-duty police officer, I noticed his gaze scanning each storefront as we passed through town. When I asked him about it, he said that he naturally scans stores for any irregularities. It is his interest and his environment. A farmer from the Midwest transplanted to a large inner city environment would be forced to quickly shift his awareness capability in order to survive.

Awareness is related to attention span and short-term memory. This gives us a basis for understanding how we can improve awareness. Through practice, you can improve short-term memory by progressively adding more and more items to a list you are memorizing. Later in this section you will have the opportunity to complete exercises to expand your awareness.

What Is Your Body Telling You?

The human body has been designed to resist an infinite number of changes and attacks brought about by its environment. The secret of good health lies in successful adjustment to changing stresses on the body.

HARRY J. JOHNSON
PHYSICIAN

Many argue that the body has its own awareness. At the very least our bodies can be barometers. Traumas from long ago are imprinted not only on the subconscious but also on the body. For example, some professionals who work on the body report that some patients—because of a childhood trauma such as sexual molestation—have areas of their bodies (maybe an arm that was consistently grabbed as the abuse session began) that are totally without feeling, similar to paralysis. If you touch the patient's arm she doesn't feel it. The professional works to open up this trauma site in the body, thereby opening up the trauma in the subconscious as well. These extreme cases point out how important awareness of our own bodies can be in effectively being attuned to our total environment.

There is research that suggests that comprehension of written material and reading speed are linked to our ability to hold our breath. In effect, we absorb chunks of information as we read. The size of the chunks of information is equivalent to the length of time we can hold our breath. Although we don't consciously hold our breath, the time between inhaling and exhaling (and vice versa) controls our attention span. The longer we can hold our breath, the more robust each chunk of information is likely to be. This enables us to grasp more complete thoughts, aiding our understanding of the material. So, proper breathing and enhanced aerobic capacity is valuable from more than just a physical perspective.

Paying attention to your breathing is a fast way to bring your awareness into the present moment. Your breath is always in the present moment, not focused in the past or the future. By focusing on your breath as an anchor, you can always come back to the present. You can simply focus on your breathing when you feel a bit out of control for a quick, soothing, calming effect that shifts your awareness to the present.

Awareness Exercise

This exercise involves watching one minute of a video or DVD. You will watch the same minute more than once, so starting at the beginning of the tape might be easiest for navigation.

1. Watch one minute of the tape.
2. Using your *Personal Brilliance Notebook*, write down as many details from the video as you can remember. Con-

sider all the senses—sight, sound, smell, and touch. For example, what was the texture of an object in the video? What would it feel like if you could touch it?

3. Re-cue the video and watch it again.

4. Note in your *Personal Brilliance Notebook* what you missed the first time.

5. Identify all of your awareness blocks. Was your mind wandering? Were you disturbed by the content of the video? Were you disturbed by some outside influence, such as a noise or a phone call?

In the next chapter, we'll deal with some of the most typical awareness blocks.

CHAPTER 5

Breaking Through Awareness BARRIERS

Be not the slave of your own past, plunge into the sublime seas, dive deep, and swim far, so you shall come back with self-respect, with new power, with an advanced experience, that shall explain and overlook the old.

RALPH WALDO EMERSON
POET AND ESSAYIST

HUMAN BEINGS have an innate ability to observe the here and now. However, black-and-white thinking, judgments, emotions, robotic behaviors, and myriad distractions interfere with this capability. What's amazing is that removing just one or two of your blocks can dramatically increase your awareness.

AWARENESS
CURIOSITY
FOCUS
INITIATIVE

The first step to breaking through awareness barriers is taking a close look at your most dominant blocks. Once you know what's interfering, you can begin to override your old programming and create an opening for greater awareness, both internally and externally.

In the last chapter you performed the one-minute video exercise. What were your awareness barriers?

Here is an example of lack of awareness in action in a business setting. The CEO of a manufacturing corporation hired me to coach one of his vice presidents, a plant manager. This executive was very astute when it came to the technical side of the business. However, his people skills were in question. Although he was making progress in shoring up the business aspects of the department, he had a very high turnover rate and morale was horrible, with frequent employee complaints including charges of verbal abuse. The vice president was developing a less than positive reputation within the company and in their marketplace as well.

The process in working with the vice president was one of two steps forward and one step back until he began to develop awareness and took responsibility for resolving the issues. This came to a head when he blamed me, his advisor, for the morale problems. He said, "Morale was fine until you started asking everyone what was wrong. Now that they're thinking about the negative, everything is a problem." Ironically, the reason I was consulted was because the negatives were obvious to most everyone, except the vice president.

I used his comment to explain and lay out the irrefutable evidence that my focus was indeed on the positives, even having prepared him to deliver a speech touting the accomplishments of his staff just the prior week. For some reason he was completely unaware of those positive activities. Once he became aware of this "minor" detail he began to take responsibility for his thought process and the way he spoke to his employees. This realization helped jar his rigid stance, causing the cloud to move away and allowing light to be shed on the issues. He started to develop self-awareness regarding how his actions contributed to the issues and how his actions could contribute to the solutions. The corrective actions were obvious for him once he developed an awareness of his role in the process.

Common Awareness Barriers

A list of common barriers follows. To help identify some of your own awareness barriers, read the brief descriptions that follow the checklist and then mark the ones that apply to you. Once you've determined your most prominent blocks, you can begin applying the strategies provided to break through those barriers.

___Automatic pilot
___Black-and-white thinking
___Discomfort with or avoidance of the truth (especially with self-awareness)
___Fear
___Judgments and biased opinions
___Regretting or idealizing what has already happened
___Worrying or fantasizing about what's to come

Automatic Pilot

> *Thinking is the hardest work there is, which is probably the reason so few engage in it.*
>
> HENRY FORD
> INDUSTRIALIST AND FOUNDER OF FORD MOTOR COMPANY

Not surprisingly, one of the most prominent barriers to awareness is operating on "automatic pilot." Robotic reactions block awareness and repel innovation because they are triggered by what has been, instead of what is or what could be.

Here are three common examples of blocked awareness:

1. Have you ever mentioned to your spouse or a co-worker that you like their new hairstyle, only to find out they had it cut weeks before you noticed?

2. Have you ever read a few paragraphs or pages of a book and realized that you had no recollection of what you just read?
3. Have you ever moved a piece of furniture, such as a dresser, but continued to go to the "old location" by habit?

In the first example, your eyes saw the difference but your mind registered what you were used to seeing instead of what was actually there.

In the second example, you were most likely thinking or worrying about something else while you were reading, or external barriers such as sights and sounds distracted you.

In the third example, both your mind and your body were responding to an old program. Similar to the first example, you were reacting in a somewhat robotic manner, rather than noticing the change.

Black-and-White Thinking

A great many people think they are thinking when they are merely re-arranging their prejudices.

WILLIAM JAMES
PSYCHOLOGIST AND AUTHOR

I have the opportunity to observe decision making in a business setting almost daily. One common barrier is black-and-white thinking. There are just two alternatives to choose from: black or white. More often than not the opportunity lies in the gray area between the two extremes.

For instance, one of my clients is a high-end print graphic artist generating product schematics and award-winning brochures. Brenda wanted to expand her business, but in order to do so she needed to bring in freelance artists. Unfortunately she had been burned a few times with poor-quality work from freelancers and was a bit gun-shy. Black-and-white thinking: Grow the business or don't grow the business. Hire freelancers or don't hire freelancers.

But what about the gray area? Brenda worked at the very high-end of her client needs, doing the most complicated graphics. Her clients farmed out the more mundane print graphic needs, such as business cards and letterhead design to others. What if Brenda pursued that business by assigning it to freelancers in order to test their capabilities on very low-risk assignments while concurrently growing her regular business? Once the freelancers proved trustworthy, Brenda could comfortably delegate more and more complex projects. The opportunity is in the gray area.

Discomfort with or Avoidance of the Truth (Especially with Self-Awareness)

The truth of the matter is that you always know the right thing to do. The hard part is doing it.

H. NORMAN SCHWARZKOPF
U.S. GENERAL

Love is blind. Think back to a failed connection. In our hopeful stage upon first meeting the potential partner there were many signs we missed—evasiveness, behaviors that didn't match with the person's story, conflicting statements, possibly a wandering eye. Because of our infatuation we avoided the truth and all the signs that would have warned us off before it was too late.

It isn't very easy to look inside ourselves as we are living our life, which is why life coaching has become so popular. Coaches can serve as a reflection for their clients, forcing an awareness of self. The American reality TV show *American*

Idol is a perfect example of people who lack self-awareness. They ignore the truth—that they are horrible singers—merely to get their chance for fifteen minutes of fame. Or consider the baseball player who is a perfectly good hitter, but consistently tries to hit home runs even though he doesn't really have the strength for it. His batting average suffers as he hits fly ball after fly ball right into the gloves of the outfielders.

Fear

> *Fears are educated into us and can, if we wish, be educated out.*
>
> KARL A. MENNINGER, M.D.
> *THE HUMAN MIND*

When we're afraid, we pull our energy and focus into our core to protect ourselves from the perceived danger. Physiologically, our blood flow moves to the core of our body, with less blood supply flowing to our extremities. Our awareness is analogous. In a difficult situation, when we need our awareness most to be expanded to the farthest reaches, we tend to shrink our awareness instead.

Fear paralyzes thought. We might be afraid of what's inside—fear of facing the truths about ourselves regarding our thoughts or feelings. Fears could be based on the external as well. What would happen if you learned something about a loved one that would significantly change the relationship? You might be afraid of losing face or looking stupid in front of others. If you are in a state of fear, awareness falters because you are living in either the past or the future. If you are overly concerned, for example, about how your colleagues are going to react to an idea of yours, your awareness sensors may not pick up on a subtle piece of information that may make the difference to help your idea succeed.

To see how fear blocks awareness we need only look to the variety of eyewitness accounts of a fear-inducing event like a robbery. Witnesses seeing the exact same event frequently describe the assailant very differently. One witness may describe a short man in his thirties wearing a blue coat while another reports a tall boy with a white coat. The physical and psychological impacts when we are in a state of fear significantly affect our awareness, causing us to miss important facts.

Judgments and Biased Opinions

Too often we enjoy the comfort of opinion
without the discomfort of thought.

JOHN F. KENNEDY
U.S. PRESIDENT

Judgments and biased opinions can be severe barriers to awareness. We all have them. How do your biases impact your awareness? Many times our biases are self-manifesting. If a supervisor has a negative bias toward an employee, there is a high likelihood that the employee will not be able to be successful. You see, the supervisor's awareness is focused on looking for the possible negatives. Therefore, at the first stumble, the supervisor's bias is reinforced.

All prejudices work on this principle. What innovations were delayed because a woman was not expected or allowed to work in certain jobs?

Have you ever stated that you dislike a particular food although you've never tried it? Do you think you dislike it because of a judgment or bias or do you actually dislike it because of experience? If it's the former you may be missing out on a new taste treat.

Regretting or Idealizing What Has Already Happened

*The past is really almost as much a work of
the imagination as the future.*

JESSAMYN WEST
AUTHOR

Evaluating and analyzing the past is extremely valuable. However, severely regretting an experience that is deemed negative or idealizing a positive past experience attaches too great an importance on the past.

A couple in their forties lived with a strong sense of regret regarding their choice to not have children earlier in their life. This sense of regret became so dominant they lost sight of opportunities to interact with children and the associated joy they perhaps may have experienced.

One of my acquaintances is the stereotypical high school athlete who is still stuck in memories of high school. He was a star, recruited by many colleges. Injury changed his plans. Unfortunately, his entire life pivots on the memories of the glory days twenty-five years ago. Rather than use this special history as a launching point, perhaps because of the disappointment, he instead compares most activities in his life to the experience long ago. His awareness is skewed because of this rearview-mirror perspective.

Worrying or Fantasizing About What's to Come

I never think of the future. It comes soon enough.

ALBERT EINSTEIN
PHYSICIST

Mindlessness in the form of a future orientation is paralyzing as well. Would you live your life differently if you had a guarantee of a future outcome? Let's say you know you are going to be killed in an automobile accident on a date in the future. Obviously, what you are aware of and pay attention to would be affected.

That's an extreme representation of what happens when we aren't living in the present. People worry about negatives or fantasize about the future and literally miss the present. Anticipating the future can focus awareness but if it replaces awareness we're heading for trouble. For example, a mother spending time with her son on his final leave before heading to war can use the situation to fully "be" with her son. Or, she can be so worried about the possible future that she squanders the time they have together.

Strategies for Breaking Through Awareness Barriers

Automatic Pilot

Discovery consists of seeing what everybody has seen and thinking what nobody has thought.

ALBERT VON SZENT-GYORGYI
BIOCHEMIST

For the next seven days, alter the route you take to work, to the gym, or to the grocery store. Pay attention to what you notice on your new routes. On the eighth day, take the route you were accustomed to using. Pretend you are going this way for the first time and be as attentive as you were while taking alternate routes. See how many new things or places you can observe that you haven't noticed before.

Take a book or magazine to a busy restaurant, park, or shopping mall. Practice holding your awareness on each word you read, while allowing the environment to take a back seat to your reading. After five minutes, switch your awareness perspective. Put down your reading material and tune in to your environment by using all of your senses. What do you hear, see, smell, taste, and/or feel?

Black-and-White Thinking

The color of truth is gray.

ANDRÉ GIDE
FRENCH CRITIC, ESSAYIST, AND NOVELIST

Look for the gray areas. Explore alternatives. Search for the compromise between positions. During the course of a week in every interaction look for the polarities. Identify the either/or, black/white alternatives. Then offer alternatives that are somewhere between the two extremes on the spectrum. The potential solutions don't need to be perfect. Just explore the possibilities. Note in your *Personal Brilliance Notebook* reactions from the others as your "gray" alternatives are revealed.

Discomfort with or Avoidance of the Truth (Especially with Self-Awareness)

It is the easiest thing in the world for a man to deceive himself.

BENJAMIN FRANKLIN
STATESMAN AND PHILOSOPHER

As a professional speaker and writer I ask for feedback all the time. My chosen critics and editors know to be as brutal as possible with the goal of creating the best possible result.

Ask for feedback. Identify a friend to critique your performance on something that you have created or chosen to purchase. You might use a work report, a craft item you created, or a new outfit you selected for an upcoming event. Instruct your friend to critique you as if he or she were the audience you will be engaged with, your boss, others on the committee, etc. Ask your friend to take the pessimist's view. The goal is not to make you feel good, but rather to create the best possible outcome. This is preparation prior to the actual performance.

How comfortable are you with your friend's criticism? Can you understand where it might be coming from? What will you do differently as a result of the critique? Is the final product better as a result?

Fear

> If pleasures are greatest in anticipation, just remember
> that this is also true of trouble.
>
> ELBERT HUBBARD
> AUTHOR AND EDITOR

Although usually the more information the better, for the next week try a news "fast." Don't read the newspaper, don't turn on CNN, and especially don't watch the local evening news. Replace the space created by giving up the news of fires, bank robberies, shootings, and accidents with information that you want to be aware of. Shape what you think about. Take control rather than letting a news producer decide for you.

While on your news fast, listen to conversations taking place that focus on the news you have missed. Observe how people are engaged in the news. Are they upset? Are they excited or exasperated? Do you have a desire to jump into the conversation? Compare your sense of calm with those wrapped up in the news. Observe any differences and note these in your *Personal Brilliance Notebook*. After going back to watching the news, refer to your notes. Are you still maintaining that sense of calm?

Judgments and Biased Opinions

The fewer the facts, the stronger the opinion.

ARNOLD H. GLASGOW
PSYCHOLOGIST

It is easy to believe and never question the premise behind a belief. Many wars started because of a belief. Historians can, years later, question the validity of the war by questioning the underlying beliefs. How about if we question our beliefs prior to taking irrevocable action?

Identify a belief or bias to work with. You might choose a pressing social issue such as your position on the death penalty, or a localized belief such as that families should always eat dinner together.

Using your *Personal Brilliance Notebook*, answer the following questions about a belief that you have:

- How did you arrive at the conclusion that forms the belief?
- What are the experiences or perceptions that helped you form the belief?
- What is the underlying premise or life principle on which your belief is based?

As you live your life, explore your beliefs by asking these questions. You don't necessarily need to change your beliefs, although you may find that you have a more robust perspective. The key is the process of asking the questions.

Regretting or Idealizing What Has Already Happened

Memory is a complicated thing, a relative to truth,
but not its twin.

BARBARA KINGSOLVER
AUTHOR

My wife is famous for breaking into song at the slightest prov-ocation. A word or sound will trigger a song, and she begins singing quietly. One holiday family dinner we noticed that she had unconsciously changed the lyrics of the Christmas carol, "Let it Snow." She was singing, "Let it go, let it go, let it go. . . ." Words to live by.

It would be unthinkable to drive your car while looking in the rearview mirror the whole time. A crash and pain are inevitable. Staying in the present will allow our receptors to pick up what is happening now.

We frequently take pictures at a special event to maintain the memories. Have you ever looked at the pictures and thought, "When did that happen?" As an exercise attend a party with a friend. After the party, compare notes. Deter-mine how many situations both of you were aware of. Deter-mine how many situations one of you missed. This exercise will hopefully enrich your experience. There is a difference between taking a picture of an event and completely experi-encing it so that you can reproduce it for yourself as well as explain it to others.

Worrying or Fantasizing About What's to Come

To know the road ahead, ask those coming back.

CHINESE PROVERB

There is a balance between staying in the present and the need for anticipation to help us perform "the next step." Only after we master staying in the present moment can we attempt the multitasking required to be fully aware now while thinking ahead to the next step.

Do what you are doing now. Just do that. Totally focus on it. If you're driving, just drive. If you are eating, just eat—no conversation, no TV, no reading, just eat. If you are having a conversation, listen, and then speak. Notice how often you are preparing your reply while the other person is speaking. Create these mini-awareness exercises throughout your day. It's quite simple. If you are present with your task at hand, you can't be in the past or the future.

*   *   *

There are many awareness exercises in the next chapter. Choose the ones that sound interesting to you. Pay attention to your awareness barriers and focus your development program around offsetting these barriers.

Keep in mind: If the bridge is out up ahead on a darkened road, our ignorance of the missing bridge won't keep us dry.

CHAPTER 6

Amplifying AWARENESS

Normal day, let me be aware of the treasure you are.

MARY JEAN IRION
WRITER AND EDUCATOR

AMPLIFYING your natural awareness gives you an edge in all areas of life. People who are highly aware are in the best position to see more of their options. Rather than moving from one scene in their lives to the next while on auto-pilot, their eyes are wide open and they can see the big picture. Their ability to "take it all in" enables them to rise above paradoxes and find solutions. It also increases their enjoyment, because more freedom of choice means less stress and more fun.

> AWARENESS
> CURIOSITY
> FOCUS
> INITIATIVE

Whereas breaking awareness barriers involves strengthening your weak spots, amplifying your awareness is all about refining and polishing what you already have going for you!

Here's an analogy to show the difference that amplifying your awareness can make: Imagine that you are standing in a maze. Your objective is to find your way out, but you have no idea how the maze is laid out and the walls are too high to climb. It could take a very long time and an incredible amount of energy to find the exit—not to mention the anxiety that a situation like this could potentially create. This is what life can be like for people who are not aware.

But for those who amplify their awareness, it's a whole different experience. In this scenario, you're walking through the maze, but you have a magical bird's-eye view and can see all of the various routes. Because of your keen awareness, you use less time and energy, and you can relax and have fun.

Jim Kemp is a founder and partner of Antaean Solutions, a consulting firm specializing in the banking industry. Jim's early career was spent at NASA as an engineer. He was part of the team in Houston responding to the now famous radio transmission from Apollo 13 astronaut Jack Swigert, "Houston, we've had a problem here." Awareness was a critical component in this significant event in the space program.

Apollo 13 commander Jim Lovell has said, "Looking back, I realize I should have been alerted by several omens that occurred in the final stages of the Apollo 13 preparation." In regard to the problematic oxygen tank during testing, Lovell says he should have said, "Hold it. Wait a second. I'm riding on this spacecraft. Just go out and replace that tank."

Jim Kemp's job as a junior engineer involved inventorying all of the contents of the Apollo spacecraft, a process that was integral to the solutions created by ground personnel to deal with the buildup of carbon-dioxide in the spacecraft. The long-distance problem-solving that got the astronauts home safely required a keen awareness of the limited tools available in the spacecraft. Knowing exactly what materials were available allowed Kemp and his fellow engineers to help the astronauts create a solution. The Apollo 13 accident and the resulting innovations that brought the astronauts home safely are a perfect example of the catalysts of awareness, curiosity, focus, and initiative at work.

Is personal brilliance just for scientists and astronauts? Phil McCrory, a hairdresser from Madison, Alabama, was watching CNN coverage of the Exxon oil spill in 1989. They repeatedly showed an image of otters covered in oil. McCrory asked, "Why can't human hair, which I sweep up each day, absorb the same way?" He did some quick experiments and found that hair wrapped up in pantyhose absorbed nearly 100 percent of the oil. After work with NASA, a patent, and a system for hairdressers all over the country to send him their clippings, he was on his way to implementation. The patent Phil McCrory obtained was sold and his idea is now being used in oil spill clean-up today. McCrory says, "I have ideas that are just wild, they seem to just fall out of nowhere." Awareness first, then curiosity, focus, and initiative led to his innovation.

Ellen DeGeneres, when asked how she was able to speak "whale" for her performance in the movie *Finding Nemo,* said she used to have a neighbor who did aerobics to a tape of whale noises at high volume. At the time, she found it upsetting. But surprisingly she was able to tap into that experience when the time came to work on the movie. Awareness.

Following are some exercises to amplify your awareness.

Increase Your Muscle Awareness

Bodies never lie.

AGNES DE MILLE
DANCER, CHOREOGRAPHER, AND WRITER

When performing daily activities, focus your awareness on your muscle tension. Which muscles are tense? Which muscles are relaxed? Where is your tongue? If it's on the roof of your mouth or sticking out à la Michael Jordan, your lower jaw may be unnecessarily tense. I recently noticed tenseness in my shoulders while washing dishes. Was I so focused on the dirty dishes that I was tensed to give the activity my all? Was how I stood contributing to the tenseness? Was I zoning out and thinking about something other than the activity of washing the dishes? Just noticing the tense shoulders allowed some minor adjustments to make the process more comfortable.

Contemplate and Consider Different Perspectives

Men are disturbed not by things, but by the views they take of them.

EPICTETUS
STOIC PHILOSOPHER

The more perspectives you consider, the more choices you will have for how to respond. But find a balance, neither clinging white-knuckled to your own views nor letting others define you and your behavior.

Being decisive is a positive trait, and too many opinions can slow things down. However, seeking different perspectives can serve to increase awareness. For your next decision allow some extra time and seek the opinions of a diverse cast of characters. Compare the opinions and see if there are any surprises. Did anyone provide a perspective you didn't think of? Did they approach the problem in a different way? You will likely find that you now have a fresh insight into the thinking of those you asked to provide input.

Practice Empathy

Resolve to be tender with the young, compassionate with the aged, sympathetic with the striving, and tolerant with the weak and wrong. Sometime in life you will have been all of these.

BOB GODDARD
BRITISH AUTHOR

You can increase your awareness by being open to others and practicing empathy. Put yourself in the other person's shoes. What were they thinking? Why did they do what they did? For practice, choose someone in an interesting situation and empathize with what they are experiencing. Perhaps there is a person fighting for a cause that you don't necessarily agree with. What makes them tick? Why do they feel so strongly about their cause? Why don't you feel the same way?

Look Closely at Processes

The work will teach you how to do it.

ESTONIAN PROVERB

Consider how and why things are done. Notice how obstacles are part of the process, not a negative to avoid. Some very important discoveries were made as someone, paying close attention to a routine process, noticed something else that led to an innovation. I was fortunate early in my career to write user procedures for various job functions. This experience trained me to identify the beginning and the end of a process and to break down the steps along the way.

As an exercise, document the steps in the process for daily activities you perform. Use your *Personal Brilliance Notebook* to describe each step in a way that others could understand. Be careful to start at the beginning. Identify what flows into the process. Describe the steps clearly and in order. Note when the process is completed. What flows out of this process to another related process? Start with simple things like your morning grooming routine and expand to more complex processes such as preparing a favorite dinner, cleaning or caring for your car, or preparing for a presentation or special event. Articulating the process leads to an opening of your awareness of the details that make things work.

Another awareness exercise relating to process is to participate in and observe an ethnic celebration—a wedding, a parade, or a festival. Try to understand the cause and effect of the traditional activities. Notice the differences from your traditions.

Peel Back the Layers

Turn yourself inside out, so you can see
yourself with fresh eyes.

JEAN-PAUL SARTRE
FRENCH WRITER AND PHILOSOPHER

When an event occurs, move your awareness beyond your initial reaction. Instead of "Oh no—here comes another problem," for example, consider what you fear. Forging new relationships? The loss of control? Changes to your routines? Having to be a novice again? Being specific shows ways you can have power over a situation.

Pay Attention to Your Breathing

What would it be like if you lived each day, each breath, as
a work of art in progress? Imagine that you are a Masterpiece
unfolding, every second of every day a work of art taking
form with every breath.

THOMAS CRUM
MARTIAL ARTS EXPERT, AUTHOR, AND "PEAK PERFORMANCE" COACH

As we discussed in Chapter 4, paying attention to your breathing is a great way to stay in the present. It's difficult to be engaged in the past or future when focusing on our breathing. There are many breathing exercise techniques available that we teach in our workshops. One very popular technique I picked up from an Aikido instructor is the six-way breath. This technique involves visualizing the flow of our breath beyond simply in and out through our nose or mouth. With a bit of practice you visualize the exhalation of breath extending from your body in six directions. In Aikido this technique is used to help the martial artist extend a 360-degree awareness to guard against attacks from any direction.

In a relaxed position, inhale deeply. Upon exhalation visualize the air leaving your body through the top of your head and extending high into the sky. On the next exhalation, visualize the breath leaving from the front of your chest. Continue visualizing exhalations from your back, each shoulder, and down through the ground. As your practice continues, start to put the exhalation directions together until you can comfortably visualize your exhalations leaving your body in all six directions. Create for yourself a force field of awareness that extends as far as you would like.

Look for Beautifully Designed Things

Every day look at a beautiful picture, read a beautiful poem, listen to beautiful music, and, if possible, say some reasonable thing.

JOHANN WOLFGANG VON GOETHE
GERMAN POET, DRAMATIST, AND NOVELIST

Look around you for beautifully designed objects, no matter how small or specialized. Let these things inspire you to be innovative in your life. These designs could be man-made or from nature. Spend a day looking for great design: your coffee mug, your toothbrush, the car, a bridge, a chair. Why are these such great designs?

Spend an hour on the next nice-weather day gazing at clouds. What images do these wonders of nature conjure for you? Let your imagination fly with the clouds.

An equally helpful awareness exercise is to analyze poorly designed products. We tend to take great design for granted, but poor design tends to come into our awareness more easily. For example, I recently rented a car with very poorly designed drink holders. The only way to get a cup into the drink holder was to put the car in gear. Once you were in motion you were fine. But when you stop and put the car in park you crush your drink cup. What were the designers thinking? What were the constraints of the designers? The exercise of thinking about the process helps us to see much more and potentially develop solutions to the design problems.

Practice Awareness

Let us not look back in anger or forward in fear,
but around in awareness.

JAMES THURBER
HUMORIST AND ILLUSTRATOR

I think of brilliant answers floating all around us. Recognizing the subtle messages, data, and perspectives we need to generate innovation is key. This requires awareness. Awareness can be amplified with practice. When faced with various situations use your senses to explore what's happening. Ask the following questions:

- Globally, what do I sense?
- What do I feel?
- What do I see?
- What do I hear?
- What do I smell?
- What do I taste?

Also, explore what's missing. For example, when you walk into your home, explore what you sense. Also, identify what might be missing. In my case, if I walked into my home and didn't hear the jingle from our Border Collie's collar as she routinely runs to greet me, I would know something was seriously wrong.

The following exercise is designed to further develop the awareness of your senses.

Heighten Your Senses

Choose a room in your house or apartment to complete this exercise:

- Sit in your selected room with your eyes closed. Balance your breathing to an equal rhythm of inhaling and exhaling and then simply notice everything that you can with your other senses.
- After about a minute, open your eyes and write down everything that you sensed without your vision.
- Put on headsets or insert earplugs and repeat the exercise with your eyes open.
- Write down what you observed, without the assistance of your hearing.
- Close your eyes and your ears. Really tune into the scent of the air. What do you smell? Notice the chair or sofa on

which you are sitting. What does the fabric feel like? Is your seat firm or soft? Notice your posture. Breathe through your mouth and see if you can taste anything in the air. Is there food cooking or can you taste the fragrance of a nearby flowering plant or tree?

- Write down what you observed with your sense of touch, taste, and smell.
- Compare your lists and see which senses are most acute for you and which ones gave you less information.
- Practice increasing your awareness of the senses that you are not fully using by repeating this exercise from time to time.

*   *   *

How aware are you as you read the words in this book? Are you analyzing how this information will positively affect your life? Have you engaged with the material or is it just an abstraction? The next section adds curiosity to your amplified awareness to assist you on your journey toward consistent innovation.

CURIOSITY

CHAPTER 7

The Power of CURIOSITY

A sense of curiosity is nature's original school of education.

SMILEY BLANTON, M.D.
LOVE OR PERISH

CURIOSITY is a vital catalyst of personal brilliance. Actively exploring the environment, asking questions, investigating possibilities, and possessing a sense of wonder are all part of being curious. In effect, curiosity is the cure for boredom!

Curiosity requires freedom—freedom from the barriers that inhibit discovery. Questions are key. Once you open up to the nuances of life, it's easy to find things that fascinate you and to begin wondering "why?" and "how?"

AWARENESS
CURIOSITY
FOCUS
INITIATIVE

Curiosity works together seamlessly with awareness, focus, and initiative. While the gift of awareness helps you assess how things are, curiosity helps you clarify problems, ideas, and situations, and it encourages you to explore how they could be different.

- When you're curious about something, your mind shifts into an investigative mode of thinking, which amplifies your awareness.
- Following the path of a question expands your focus because each bit of information that you gather gives a greater perspective.

• Curiosity can get you going! There's nothing like a burning question to trigger your initiative.

Curiosity jump-starts personal brilliance. Questioning takes you to deeper levels of knowing and helps you relate to others. When you develop heightened curiosity, you improve the quality of your life by asking better questions and being receptive to new ideas. The desire to expand your understanding motivates you to go beyond the surface. You *learn more* because you have a desire to *know more*. When you approach an idea, person, or situation with a heightened sense of curiosity, your natural tendency is to "quest" for additional information. Even when you can't immediately apply what you learn, you are training to keep your curiosity muscles "buff."

Another advantage of being curious is that your brain is designed to reward you for exploring fresh ideas and trying new activities. When you experience novelty, your brain produces more dopamine—an important brain chemical that lifts your mood and increases your sense of well-being.

How Did They Do That?

Curiosity is the wick in the candle of learning.

WILLIAM A. WARD
PROFESSOR AND EGYPTOLOGIST

Have you ever wondered, "How did they do that?"

For example, you know that Henry Ford was an innovator. After all, he built the Ford Motor Company and played a big part in developing mass-production techniques for our most common mode of transportation. But what you might not know is that curiosity was a critical catalyst in the early stages of Ford's innovations.

As the story goes, Ford was attending a French automobile race and witnessed a crash on the track. His curiosity got the best of him and he left the grandstand to take a closer look at the wreckage. As he sifted through the pieces and parts, he was surprised how light they were. Solely because of his curiosity, he learned about "vanadium," the strong, lightweight metal alloy that was used in the racecar. Because of vanadium's strength relative to its weight, Ford was able to solve a major production problem. This coincidental discovery allowed Ford to produce 15 million Model-Ts!

But wait just a second. Was this discovery really just a coincidence?

There were hundreds of people at the race. Likely, they all filed out of the stands and went about their business after the race was over. Henry Ford's simple curiosity—wondering what happened and what he might learn from closer examination—led to a major innovation affecting almost every person on the planet. I'll bet he didn't even know exactly what he was looking for in that wreckage. But curiosity led him there to discover the hidden treasure.

Curiosity in Action

Man's mind stretched to a new idea never goes
back to its original dimensions.

OLIVER WENDELL HOLMES, SR.
PHYSICIAN, AUTHOR AND POET

My graphic artist, Arnie Friedlander, and I were at the print shop reviewing a new poster when Arnie disappeared. A few minutes later I found him sitting on the floor of the pressroom in a pile of scrap paper. The sheets were scrapped because the press had accidentally printed multiple photos on top of each other on each page. Arnie, with the curiosity of a child, sat with the scraps and said, "Look at this. These images piled on top of each other make you wonder what's beneath the surface. I can use this concept."

It's not surprising that Arnie wins awards for his commercial artwork. His heightened level of curiosity gives him an edge. He hones that edge by putting all four catalysts of personal brilliance to work.

Ask Questions

It is important that students bring a certain ragamuffin,
barefoot irreverence to their studies; they are not here to
worship what is known, but to question it.

JACOB BRONOWSKI
BRITISH SCIENTIST AND AUTHOR

Without new questions there are no new answers.

As a professional speaker and active member of the National Speakers Association, I have the privilege of sitting in on many speeches. I am most intrigued by the traditional question-and-answer period. Frequently, after an hour-long presentation when it's time to take questions, there aren't any. This astonishes me. If the presentation was interesting and engaging, there must be hundreds of questions about the basis for the ideas, how to implement them, and the next steps to take. Even if the presentation wasn't so hot, there are scores of possible questions of a challenging nature to discover a better approach to ingesting the information.

There are many reasons for this "no questions" phenomenon. Nervousness in front of a group, fear of looking foolish, and not wanting to show off in front of peers are just a few. The biggest problem is that we train ourselves to repress questions. After all, if we're not going to voice the questions because of all the unpleasant social issues, why bother coming up with questions at all? By acting in this manner, we are effectively reinforcing the opposite of the habit of curiosity.

Curiosity Exercise #1

At the next presentation you attend, write down three questions that dig deeper into the subject matter. Since you are fighting social pressures, you don't have to actually ask the questions. However, at a future presentation, commit to raising your hand and asking a question or two. See what happens.

Dig Deeper

The only way of discovering the limits of the possible is to venture a little way past them into the impossible.

ARTHUR C. CLARKE
PROFILES OF THE FUTURE

The depth of questioning is also important. Many times digging past the first or obvious answer is necessary to generate innovation. For instance, The Kimberly-Clark Company wants to know what their customers want. This company listens to what their customers say and digs deeper to discover what they really mean. It was this habit of deeper questioning that resulted in the development of "pull-up" training pants for toddlers. Kimberly-Clark listened beyond the mere words to hear parents' wishes that their kids feel grown-up even though they are still in diapers. In this case, curiosity led to millions of dollars in profit.

Curiosity Exercise #2

Whether you have a traditional job or not, it's important to keep your resume up to date. Don't update your resume only when you anticipate being downsized or you just can't take it anymore. Many personal development gurus suggest that you update your resume constantly, and I agree. Remember that you can't get the right answers without the right questions. While updating your resume, here are some questions to keep in the forefront of your mind:

1. My major task/project for this week is challenging me in the following way/s: _____.

2. In the last three months I learned _____.

3. The most important addition to my personal network in the past three months is _____.

4. What makes me uniquely valuable is _____.

5. Others think of me when they think of _____.

6. By next year they will also think of me when they think of _____.

Wonder and Doubt

To believe with certainty, we must begin with doubting.

STANISLAUS I LESZCZYNSKI
KING OF POLAND

In terms of innovation, questions come in two basic forms—wonder and doubt. The questions of wonder come from not knowing or not having been exposed to something before. Innovation can spring from a question based in wonder because this type of curiosity looks at something from a new perspective.

A great example of achieving success through a sense of wonder is the high school student in Lincoln, New Hampshire, who successfully cloned the rare orchid plant Lady's Slipper. April Dovoluk didn't know that the plant was notoriously difficult to transplant, and nearly impossible to grow from seed. She also didn't know that scientists had been trying to clone Lady's Slipper for years without any success. She simply knew that the plant was on the endangered list, thought it was pretty, and felt it would be a good idea to help it spread. April's success astonished the orchid world. April and two fellow students on the project, Tyler King and Katie Sokolski, won second prize at the prestigious 1996 International Science and Engineering Fair.

The questions of doubt come from knowing and then challenging with a question. In order to ask questions that generate innovation, you need to entertain doubts. Without doubt, there can be no learning and there can be no progress. If the student is not permitted to doubt the teacher, there is a limit placed upon the learning. The ego of the teacher must allow for doubt—often a scary allowance when faced with forty teenagers or a room full of CEOs. This applies to any teacher, boss, supervisor, or parent. If doubt isn't promoted, the teaching session may be completed, but true learning may not occur.

A good case in point is powered human flight in the 1950s, where success resulted in large part because of doubt. An entire base of knowledge was generated concerning flight and the related disciplines: aerodynamics, physics, metallurgy, and engine design. Based on this body of knowledge, certain ideas about what was possible took shape. For example, according to what we "knew," we could not fly fast enough to break the sound barrier. Experts said that at the speed of sound, propellers would disintegrate and wings would fall off. This was true, based on the science of the time. Fortunately, someone doubted the commonly accepted wisdom—namely that it was impossible to fly faster. New designs using the proper scientific laws, rather than the currently accepted laws, were necessary. Without healthy doubt, curiosity shuts down and innovation does not occur.

Although difficult, if we can accept that we are not absolutely sure of anything, we can allow productive doubt to flourish. It's wonderful that someone doubted that man can't fly, that we can't communicate instantly over large distances, and that we are at the mercy of diseases like the plague.

As human beings, "knowing" the answers helps us to feel in control of our lives. However, it is through suspending our beliefs and questioning our knowledge that we make true advances in our life and the lives of others.

Curiosity Helps You Really Learn

People learn something every day, and a lot of times it's that what they learned the day before was wrong.

BILL VAUGHAN
AUTHOR AND JOURNALIST

What do you know? I mean, what do you really know? As Nobel Laureate physicist Richard P. Feynman said, "Knowing the name of something and knowing something are two different things. If you know the name of a bird, you only know what other people call it. What do you know about the bird?" We live at such a frantic pace, learning can serve as a pleasant way to stop and smell the roses. Curiosity can help you notice more detail about your surroundings. Don't settle for knowing just the name. Really learn about it.

Curiosity Exercise #3

Take a moment to study your hand. The human hand is a marvel of engineering. Wonder how it grasps objects, why the knuckles are placed where they are, and how its size, relative to the rest of your body, affects its use. Explore your hand's range of motion and rotation. Question why there are little hairs on the back of the hand, but not on your palm. Theorize about why you have fingerprints. You get the idea. Really learn about the hand. Get past the label and explore completely. Then go to the next step. How can you use the information in other areas of your life? This same type of curiosity motivated the famous inventors throughout history.

Research and discovery can be learned just like any other skills. The World Wide Web and the hyperlinks that allow you to dig deeper into related subjects are a perfect analogy to describe how curiosity can work. A curiosity practice session should be very unstructured. Don't place a time limit on your work. Wonder and wander. Let the information you discover guide you to the next step. Get wrapped up in the activity of learning. Ask the next question, and the next question. Over time, you will be able to generate questions and answers more quickly and fit your research into required timeframes.

Are You Too Old to Learn?

You will stay young as long as you learn, form new habits
and don't mind being contradicted.

Marie von Ebner-Eschenbach
Austrian author

I regularly hear people say that they're too old to learn. They say they are at the stage of their lives where they just don't want to know any more. Politeness requires that I repress my desire to shake them. Only 35 percent of Americans have read a book since graduating high school. Only 20 percent say they have ever been in a bookstore. Why do people want to stop learning? Have you ever said, "I don't need to know that?"

Learning can and should continue until the very end of our lives. A great example of life-long learning in action is the Senior Theatre Association. This organization represents senior citizens throughout the world who are members of theater companies. The membership is quite diverse. Members may have acted once in their high school play and then after retirement renewed their interest. Or, perhaps after being dragged to a play, they may have become involved with set design, costumes, or props. Some of them are even retired Broadway actors. These thespians know that the process of learning their lines, building sets, and rehearsing their roles keeps them young.

Actress Birdie Larrick suffered a stroke while performing one evening. She completed her performance. After all, the show must go on. Following a short hospital stay and some physical therapy she was right back at it within a few weeks, and she was as sharp as ever. She attributes her ability to bounce back to her intense curiosity and desire to do something new and learn from the experience, even at the age of 82.

Marilyn, an acquaintance I met at a social function, is a veteran high school physical education and health teacher, with twenty years of experience in an inner city school environment. I was astounded by what she told me in our first conversation. She told me she only read what she needed to learn, and if it doesn't apply directly to her, she doesn't want to know about it. Someone who teaches our children was telling me she didn't care to learn.

I was curious about her motivations and what caused her to feel this way. I asked about her youthful idealism when she started as a teacher. We continued our discussions and began to work together in a coaching relationship. I asked Marilyn a number of questions that caused her to reexamine her life and her goals. As a result of the personal brilliance material and exercises she began to have a more expansive view of her possibilities.

Marilyn, while recognizing the importance of her work as a teacher, decided she wanted to help many more people than she can reach in her classes. Marilyn began to research the possibilities that would allow her to continue reaching her students at an even deeper level, while also influencing better teaching practices within her school, school system, and ultimately throughout the state.

Marilyn began to research what was possible. Her reading load increased exponentially with little stress because Marilyn shifted back into a learning mode. Learning, and learning about teaching, was fun again. This sense of curiosity has changed Marilyn's outlook. Her excitement came out as she asked questions of school administrators and leaders of various school programs. The fire was lit and people took notice. Marilyn was offered an opportunity to pilot a new program that educates physical education teachers on new methods to use in the classroom. She has been very successful, speaking and training throughout the country, having a positive impact on thousands of students while still doing an even better job for her local students.

Whatever your age, curiosity can lead you off the beaten path into exciting new territory. Steve Wilson is the founder of the World Laughter Tour. For many years, Steve practiced as a psychologist while building a professional speaking career around the subject of using humor and laughter in the heath care professions. At about the time Steve was slowing down his practice he decided to take advantage of an opportunity to do a speaking tour in India. Why? He was curious how his ideas might be accepted in a totally different culture.

While there, Steve experienced the concept of laughter clubs, which existed throughout India. Steve became very curious about the concept and his desire to learn more about it prompted him to invite a practitioner to the U.S. so he could observe how this concept could be applied in North America. Steve's curiosity, along with the other catalysts of innovation, has resulted in a phenomenon that is sweeping through North America's long-term therapeutic care facilities. Steve's curiosity led to opportunities he didn't even know existed. His quest for more and better information is having a significant impact on his life and the lives of many others. Curiosity pays off.

Curiosity Quest

The whole art of teaching is only the art of awakening the natural curiosity of young minds for the purpose of satisfying it afterwards.

ANATOLE FRANCE
FRENCH AUTHOR

What was the last idea or topic that you researched, just because you wanted to learn more about it?

For me, it was thoroughbred racehorse breeding. While I have no intention of breeding horses, one of my friends was getting into this new business and I participated in his learning curve just because it was interesting. Questing for information, even when it doesn't seem to be pertinent, will enhance the curiosity that may be lying dormant within you. I didn't exercise my curiosity with the intention of directly benefiting from the information, but my newfound knowledge of horse breeding and racing has opened the door to some new business relationships. That's the funny thing about knowledge. You often don't recognize the benefit of what you've learned until you've learned it.

Curiosity Exercise #4

Part 1

Here's a challenge for you. Write down a question that has piqued your curiosity. It might be general, such as, "How are clouds formed?" Or, it could be very specific, such as, "What do I need to do to get the promotion I want?" Spend one hour finding the answer to your question.

Part 2

When time is up, use the Curiosity Checklist below to identify the research areas you used in your quest. Based on the checklist, is there something else you want to investigate?

Curiosity Checklist

1. *Check the resources you have on hand*
   ___Dictionary
   ___Encyclopedia
   ___Telephone book/Yellow Pages

___Books and tapes
___Maps and guidebooks
___Internet search
___Memory and personal experience

2. *Check with people who have experience in the area you're researching*
   ___Family, friends, acquaintances, and co-workers
   ___Industry experts
   ___College and university professors
   ___Groups and organizations
   ___Professional practitioners, such as doctors, lawyers, etc.

Once you have covered your options in #1 and #2, conclude your quest with #3.

3. *Checks and Balances*
   ___Look for information that conflicts with what you have found.
   ___Share what you've discovered with a few people who know nothing about the topic you are researching. Children can be wonderful resources for honest, to the point, feedback.
   ___Facilitate your own focus group to see how others respond to your findings.
   ___Conduct a survey to see how others respond to the questions you're exploring.

*   *   *

The power that comes from heightening your curiosity is truly unlimited. When you put judgments aside, you can come up with some of your most brilliant ideas. One of my favorite stories that illustrates the essence of asking high-quality questions is a parable of sorts that I heard Dr. James E. Loehr tell in his *Mental Toughness Training* audio program. The story involves a court jester and his king.

The court jester's role in the kingdom was to amuse the king and his court. He was the only person in the land who was permitted to poke fun at the king. He made an art of asking himself questions that led to clever ideas for songs and skits. One day, however, he went too far in making fun of the king and the king sentenced him to death. The king's advisors pleaded with him to show mercy to the court jester who had served him well for many years.

The king called the jester before him and said, "I cannot rescind my order for your death, but I can show you mercy by permitting you to choose the way you want to die."

If the jester would have responded based on what he had seen previously, he most likely would have asked for a "quick and painless death." But this man had been honing his curiosity skills for many years. Instead of falling back on dogmatic beliefs, he paused to ponder the question more deeply. Finally, the jester responded, "Given the choice, your majesty, I choose to die of old age."

CHAPTER 8

Why? Thinking Like a CHILD

The young do not know enough to be prudent, and therefore they attempt the impossible—and achieve it, generation after generation.

PEARL S. BUCK
NOVELIST

COLE is three and a quarter. His mom and dad have just left for an evening out. Cole is a bit despondent because he's stuck with his sitter Uncle Jim for the evening. In Cole's mind the worst-case scenario is that his parents have abandoned him. At best, they are off doing something fun and he's being left out. He decides to sprawl on the stairs and pout. Most experienced parents know that there is no direct way to reverse this scenario. Curiosity to the rescue.

AWARENESS
CURIOSITY
FOCUS
INITIATIVE

I simply ignored Cole and his pouting and began preparing dinner. About two minutes into the process Cole's curiosity overtook his angst. I suddenly heard, "What are you doing, Uncle Jim?" Cole used his finely honed climbing skills to scurry up onto the kitchen island to closely examine the process of slicing the bright red tomatoes into the salad. The questions began: Why are the tomatoes so small? Where do tomatoes come from? What are the green things on top of the tomatoes? Can I taste one? Can

I taste another one? Why are you putting salt on them? You get the idea.

Natural curiosity bubbled from Cole and his state of mind dramatically changed. Cole has yet to develop the unfortunate adult ability to overcome his natural curiosity. Because of his curiosity, he moved from a mental state close to depression to one of excitement based in learning. Cole shifted from thoughts anchored in the past (my mom and dad left) to the present (what's happening here and now). Perhaps adults could simulate this natural child-like approach to mental health?

You're Born with Curiosity

If you've ever spent time with a young child, you know that curiosity is a natural gift. Children are like miniature reporters, constantly asking who, what, when, where, and particularly why. They also have very few preconceived notions, so they are open to taking in new information without being constrained by biases and judgments. An exchange with the seven-year-old daughter of a friend highlights this openness. She said, "My mom told me not to talk to strangers." I agreed that her mother had given her savvy advice. But then she asked, "What is a stranger?" I easily replied, "A stranger is someone you don't know." She thought for a moment and replied, "But I didn't know any of my friends when I met them, so they were all strangers, weren't they?" What could I say? She had me. In that moment, I realized that thinking like a child opened doorways that most adults had closed years before.

An important part to heightening your curiosity is to observe children and allow yourself to return to childlike thinking when you are facing an opportunity, challenge, or problem. When faced with a situation that requires enhanced curiosity, I eat lunch at a local restaurant that overlooks an interactive dancing fountain. Children play and dance with the water while trying to figure out the fountain's patterns. This simple act (I have to eat somewhere) opens up the wonder that lies within. I tend to ask better questions after seeing the children experiment with and embrace the world in which they live.

A UCLA study showed that at the age of five, we "engage in creative tasks 98 times a day, laugh 113 times, and ask questions 65 times. By the age of 44, however, the numbers shrink to two creative tasks a day, eleven laughs, and six questions." Six questions compared to sixty-five questions per day! Are we really so wise at age 44 that we don't have any questions? Or, instead, are we so used to taking shortcuts based on preconceived judgments for the sake of expediency that questions and the resulting answers are replaced by assumptions and models based on past experience?

How can adults take advantage of the natural child-like curiosity that is stripped away as we learn to identify risks and determine how things cannot be done? Henry Ford made a commitment to develop an "unbreakable" glass for car windshields. When Ford's highly educated engineers reported that it was "impossible" to make this type of windshield, Ford directed them to find someone who didn't know it was impossible. The plant recruited some curious engineers who had not yet accumulated a mass of limitations based on what they "knew," and this group came up with the formula to manufacture shatterproof glass. A commitment to curiosity solved a seemingly impossible problem and has saved scores of lives in the decades since this innovation was introduced.

Curiosity Exercise #1

Part 1

Remember the analysis of how your hand works in the last chapter? How many questions can you ask about how the hand works? In your *Personal Brilliance Notebook* list as many questions as you can—at least ten questions.

Part 2

Choose a topic that is more directly linked to your life, perhaps an aspect of your job or a relationship. Repeat the process. List as many questions as possible.

First list the questions. There is no need to answer them until you can't come up with any more questions. After your initial questions are listed, begin to answer each one. What further questions are implied in your answers? Try this exercise when you're stuck, or as you are addressing problems or challenges. The question process can create just the right amount of openness to infuse your problem-solving process.

Part 3

What are the ten most important questions in your life right now? In your *Personal Brilliance Notebook*, list as many questions as you can in one sitting. These questions can range from, "Why are pencils no longer made with lead?" to "How can I best contribute to humanity?" Identify the top ten questions from your list. Review these questions regularly. Seek opinions from others.

Why? The Root Cause

It is not enough to have a good mind.
The main thing is to use it well.

RENÉ DESCARTES
LE DISCOURS DE LA METHODE

Another trait of children is their endless patience with the question "why." They can repeatedly ask "why" until the adults, on the edge of a breakdown, end the game with the answer, "Because I said so." When solving a problem, it's useful to determine whether, in fact, we are working with the root cause of the problem or merely a symptom. The *why* question is the key to making this determination. Usually, five *why* questions are necessary to get to the root cause.

Here's an example: Let's say the problem posed is that retail sales of our consumer product have slowed down. The problem is stated like this: "Fix the slow sales problem."

Q1: *Why* are sales of our product slowing?

A: Consumers are selecting our competitor's new product.

Q2: *Why* are consumers choosing the competitor's product over ours?

A: There is a lot of buzz about the competitor's product.

If we stop here the proposed solution may be to increase our advertising budget. But if we go deeper . . .

Q3: *Why* are the press and public so interested in the new product?

A: The competitor's product has a new feature that is billed as making it easier to use than ours.

Q4: *Why* don't we have that feature?

A: We thought it would cost too much to engineer it at the time we developed our product and guessed that the consumer was not necessarily interested in that feature. Also, there were no competitors at the time.

Q5: *Why* did we let cost dictate how our product appears in the market place?

A: Because cost savings were stated as the boss's #1 priority in the annual company meeting.

I wonder whether the CEO in this case consciously decided to lose market share when she made her speech at the company meeting.

Now that we know what the real problem is, we can take a number of actions to fix it. We're still working on the stated problem, "Fix the slow sales problem." But, we're taking actions that will address the situation directly. We're looking at the entire system that is in place that causes the situation of slower sales to occur.

This approach is useful in problem solving because it's not unusual for each person working on the problem to have a different perspective. The marketing person thinks the problem lies in manufacturing, and the engineer thinks the cause is a sales problem. Asking *why* helps take blaming out of the equation. For each person's thoughts about the problem, ask *why* until the actual cause of the problem emerges.

Let's look at a more personal situation. As evidenced by the huge market for diet and fitness products, many people aren't comfortable with their bodies. No approach works for everyone because the needs of each person are unique and the underlying motivations are sometimes hard to identify. Here's an example:

Jill says emphatically, "I hate my body."

Q1:   *Why* do you hate your body?
A: Because I'm fat, can't fit into my favorite clothes, and don't have the energy I used to have.

Q2:   *Why* do you think these changes have occurred?
A: I gained weight after childbirth, I eat fast food, and I haven't been exercising.

Q3: *Why* do you eat fast food and not exercise?

A: I'm a busy mother and the schedule for the kids and the house dominates. I don't have time.

Q4: *Why* don't you have control of your schedule?

A: To be a good mother the needs of my children have to come first.

Q5: *Why* do other needs, although important, come before your health?

A: It's the way I was taught to do it.

OK, now we have something to work with. Once we get to the core of what Jill is struggling with, she can design a program that addresses the whole issue. Without this knowledge, she may simplify the solution by trying to use willpower to avoid fast food restaurants or buying an infomercial exercise machine. You see, until Jill could determine that her sense of duty far overwhelmed her sense of self she could try every combination weight loss/fitness program with only spotty results at best. Until she could see the base issue—that she hasn't tied her personal health to her mission as a great parent—she did not have the internal drive and motivation for a sustainable solution to her problem.

What If . . . ?

It is not always by plugging away at a difficulty and sticking to it that one overcomes it; often it is by working on the one next to it. Some things and some people have to be approached obliquely, at an angle.

ANDRÉ GIDE
FRENCH CRITIC, ESSAYIST, AND NOVELIST

One technique that can be helpful to spur a new wave of questions is to ask, "What if . . . ?" relative to your challenge. This can lead to innovation by allowing you to see different perspectives. In my executive advisory work I am frequently put in the position of spokesperson in a negotiation or scenario where a party must be influenced toward a particular position. The best way to prepare is to continuously ask *What if* questions. *What if* the other party takes position A? *What if* they take position B instead? When we discuss a particular option, *what if* they react negatively? Positively?

I've been accused of being paranoid by colleagues during this type of preparation. However, it's much better to ask the questions and be prepared, than to be surprised. *What if* questions allow you to see the other viewpoint, eliminating assumptions. We are simulating the aspect of children's curiosity in which they make no assumptions about a situation. They don't assume they know. So, they ask questions.

With any technique there should be balance. Place a time limit on "what-iffing" to avoid spiraling out of control.

As World War II approached, U.S. President Franklin Roosevelt became keenly aware of the strategic importance of diamonds. Diamonds were critical in tools necessary to build the weapons of war. Without a regular supply of diamonds for industrial use, the war machine would grind to a halt. Naturally, the Axis powers were just as interested in this treasured industrial resource.

Diamond suppliers were supporting the Germans in the war. After trying unsuccessfully to secure the millions of carats of diamonds necessary to support the American war effort and finding that the Germans were somehow receiving all the diamonds they needed, it was time for some innovation.

President Roosevelt asked a *what if* question. Industry could find no other substance that met the same exacting characteristics that diamonds provided. *What if* we could make our own diamonds? Could we simulate the actions of Mother Nature when producing diamonds?

The invention of processes to manufacture an unlimited supply of industrial-grade diamonds was the result of this *what if* question. Another example of how an innovation based in curiosity has shaped the future of the world.

Look Beyond the Obvious

Never assume the obvious is true.

WILLIAM SAFIRE
SLEEPER SPY

As an exercise, it's sometimes helpful to look beyond the obvious. Otherwise, we fall victim to the cliché of not seeing the forest for the trees. An acquaintance of mine, who used to read electric meters, said that looking beyond the obvious saved him from being bitten by dogs several times.

He said when he first started reading meters, he'd look to see if a dog was free in the yard and if not, he'd walk up to read the meter. It seemed obvious enough—until the day a large black dog appeared out of nowhere and knocked Bill to the ground. Fortunately, it was an overly friendly Black Labrador, who proceeded to lick Bill's face as if they were long-lost friends. Bill said, "After that, I learned that just because I don't see a dog doesn't mean there isn't a dog. I look for other signs now, like paths through the yard, toys, bones, and water bowls."

The obvious can mask information that may be vital to learning the truth of a situation. The huge face of the "Great and Powerful Wizard of Oz" hovering in mid-air and speaking sternly to Dorothy and her friends kept everyone but Toto from noticing the curtained booth where the man behind the voice was hiding.

The next time you catch yourself thinking, writing, or saying, "Obviously . . ." make a note of your assumption. Then invest a few hours in looking beyond what appears to be true. Keep searching until you find at least three pieces of information or sources that conflict with what you classified as "obvious."

Forget What You Know

Whoever undertakes to set himself up as a judge of truth and knowledge is shipwrecked by the laughter of the gods.

ALBERT EINSTEIN
PHYSICIST

Many times our knowledge gets in the way of brilliant solutions. We know too much. Part of learning is trial and error. If you've been working on something for a while with no solution, think about the failed attempts of Henry Ford's engineers who declared shatterproof glass impossible. Can you forget what you know? How about simulating the environment of Ford's new batch of engineers who naively didn't know that the innovation was impossible?

Identify the Most Impossible Solutions

What we need are more people who specialize in the impossible.

THEODORE ROETHKE
POET

When faced with a challenge, try to identify the most absurd solutions possible. This can be a fun exercise and may unmask a solution. This process tends to expose the boundary lines in our thinking. One client, for instance, was having trouble recruiting employees to his Midwest headquarters. One impossible solution was to open an office where most of the candidates were—in this case, on the East Coast. This "impossible" solution, once voiced, was actually considered.

When Everything Was Possible

*I have learned to use the word impossible with
the greatest of caution.*

WERNHER VON BRAUN
GERMAN ROCKET PIONEER

Young children believe that most everything is possible. Until someone convinces them otherwise, or until they become jaded through failures or disappointments, the world is a wide-open place filled with delightful possibilities. They can imagine flowers that talk and spaceships that shrink down small enough to fit under their bed. Nothing is off limits. To reconnect with that open sense of possibility is one of the most powerful benefits of heightening your natural gift of curiosity. Making it a practice to think like this, at least a few times each day, can trigger countless ideas for personal innovation.

CHAPTER 9

Breaking Through Curiosity BARRIERS

Be curious always! For knowledge will not acquire you; you must acquire it.
SUDIE BACK
SOCIAL PSYCHOLOGIST

WHAT STOPS US from being curious when "the desire to understand" is clearly an inborn attribute of being human?

The answer to this question is somewhat different for everyone, but there are some common curiosity barriers that many people come up against. These barriers include fear of the unknown, entrenched beliefs, insecurity, apathy, and avoidance. The magic with curiosity is that once you start to break through the barriers, you can quickly return to a state of child-like wonder and questioning.

AWARENESS
CURIOSITY
FOCUS
INITIATIVE

These are two common examples of blocked curiosity:

- Have you ever been tantalized by a question, but have written it off as "folly" because you believed that it wasn't possible to find an answer or solution?
- Have you ever stopped yourself from pursuing a question because you were afraid of what you might find out?

In the first example, your natural instinct was to question, but your mind stopped the process by insisting that you could not find an answer, or by thinking that there is no answer.

In the second example, you stopped your inquiry because on some level you believed that you were not ready, willing, or able to handle the answers that might result from your quest.

Let's begin by assessing your most prominent curiosity blocks. Once you determine your barriers, you can begin to transcend those limitations and create an internal atmosphere that is ripe for greater curiosity.

Common Curiosity Barriers

Here is a list of common curiosity barriers. To identify your own curiosity barriers, read the brief descriptions that follow the checklist and then mark the ones that apply to you. Once you've determined your dominant blocks, you can begin applying the strategies provided to break through those barriers.

___Apathy or indifference

___Desire to avoid "what is" or "what may be"

___Dogmatic belief that what you "know" is true

___Fear of the unknown

___Insecurity or feeling of inadequacy

___Myth that an answer or better approach can't be found

Apathy or Indifference

> *The biggest temptation is to settle for too little.*
>
> THOMAS MERTON
> RELIGIOUS WRITER AND POET

"I just don't care."

Everyone has certain interests that give them a charge.

Unfortunately, it's not possible to address only the things that interest us. You've probably experienced this at work. There may be a task or project that just wasn't your cup of tea. Or perhaps you had to take a class in school because it was a required course. How effective were you in performing these tasks? While it's good advice to identify areas of life you are truly interested in for your vocation, it's not always possible to do only what we love. However, there is value to be found in every activity. If apathy or indifference cause you to not be fully engaged you may miss an important lesson or impetus to a brilliant idea.

For those with finely toned curiosity muscles, the content doesn't really matter. We are curious about anything we encounter. Many times a brilliant idea stems from a seemingly unrelated and—on the face of it—not very interesting area.

Desire to Avoid "What Is" or "What May Be"

Many things cause pain, which would cause pleasure
if you regarded their advantages.

BALTASAR GRACIAN Y MORALES
THE ART OF WORLDLY WISDOM

"What if I don't get the answer I want?" or "What if it's bad news?" It is natural to avoid pain or a negative situation. The problem is that until we do the exploration we're simply guessing about a negative result. Should we avoid asking the question simply because we may not be comfortable with the answer? Most treatment advances in modern medicine rely on early detection. The patients who are aware of symptoms but don't seek treatment because of what may be wrong could in fact cause their worst fears to come true. Even if the symptoms turn out to be nothing, the worry time has a negative impact on their lives.

Dogmatic Belief that What You "Know" Is True

*A cup is useful only when it is empty; and a mind that is
filled with beliefs, with dogmas, with assertions, with
quotations is really an uncreative mind.*

JIDDU KRISHNAMURTI
INDIAN PHILOSOPHER

The myths that we embrace as true are some of the greatest
barriers to open-minded curiosity. John F. Kennedy said,
"The great enemy of truth is very often not the lie—deliberate,
contrived, and dishonest—but the myth—persistent, persua-
sive, and unrealistic." Being stuck in your present knowledge
and beliefs blocks curiosity and repels innovation because
you get in the way of new and different possibilities.

Curiosity requires openness. There is no reason to seek an
answer if you believe you already know the answer. Thankfully, Christopher Columbus allowed for the possibility of a
different answer than his contemporaries regarding the shape
of the world. Thankfully, mental health professionals were
curious enough to find alternatives to institutionalizing patients with what today are treatable illnesses.

Fear of the Unknown

Nothing in life is to be feared. It is only to be understood.

MARIE CURIE
POLISH-BORN FRENCH PHYSICIST

Fear of the unknown is a barrier to curiosity. Interestingly,
this is quite a paradox. Being curious and answering questions
will make the unknown known. The solution is in fact within
the question. Many times exploring the unknown is not safe.
It could be a bit scary. Growth could be painful. However,
think back to your life experience. What difficulties have you

had because of something you didn't know? Ignorance is truly not bliss. Recall my definition of success at the very beginning of this book—having choices. Without knowledge, without understanding, our choices are limited.

Insecurity or Feeling of Inadequacy

Even the people we most admire often feel inadequate.

ANDREW MATTHEWS
ARTIST, CARTOONIST, AND AUTHOR

A feeling of insecurity or inadequacy can be a barrier to curiosity because we may ignore a question, thinking we should already know the answer. I see this phenomenon many times in a group brainstorming situation. Those of lower rank within the pecking order of the group have a feeling that their natural concerns or questions have already been asked by the more experienced participants. Additionally, valid questions aren't pursued because of the fear of appearing inadequate. No matter the cause, the unasked questions are usually a barrier to a brilliant solution.

Myth that an Answer or Better Approach Can't Be Found

Argue for your limitations and sure enough they're yours.

RICHARD BACH
ILLUSIONS

"There is no answer," or "This problem has been around forever," or "We've tried solutions before to no avail." This barrier causes us to give up on solving the problem before we even begin. If you believe there is no answer then that is almost a guarantee that you won't find one. Many historical innovations were preceded by naysayers who were convinced that there was no answer. Of course, they were proven wrong. What might have been if in these situations everyone had had the courage and perseverance to pursue the questions and answers, as did Wilbur and Orville Wright or Thomas Edison?

Strategies for Breaking Through Curiosity Barriers

Apathy or Indifference

> More good things in life are lost by indifference
> than ever were lost by active hostility.
>
> ROBERT GORDON MENZIES
> AUSTRALIAN PRIME MINISTER

It's much easier to practice curiosity in relationship to something we are interested in. What jazzes you? What are you excited to learn more about? Practice with that topic and slowly expand to other topics you encounter through your day.

Capture the emotions you have when in a curious state. How do you feel? Are you excited? Do you have a sense of, "I can't wait to learn more?" Does time seem to just fly by as you explore? Make notes about how you feel in this state of mind. Now, relating to a different topic that may not be as interesting to you, try to replicate the physical and psychological patterns when addressing this new topic. In other words, pretend. Simulated motivation can be just as powerful as genuine motivation.

Perhaps you can jump-start your curiosity simply by trying to find out why other people are interested in a particular topic. If you reviewed a comprehensive list of associations, you would find an enormous diversity of topics that people are so interested in that they officially gather together to study and discuss them. There are groups of people intensely interested in everything from putting together scrapbooks to eating at every revolving restaurant in the world. I wonder why?

Desire to Avoid "What Is" or "What May Be"

It is not because things are difficult that we do not dare;
It is because we do not dare that they are difficult.

SENECA
SPANISH-BORN ROMAN STATESMAN AND PHILOSOPHER

Just about everyone has an example of a time they dreaded finding out the answer to a question, practically made themselves sick with worry, and then discovered they had nothing to fear after all. And, most of us know someone who chose to wait to ask important questions and suffered more dire consequences as a result.

Putting off knowing doesn't stop a problem from existing or progressing. The key is to be willing to ask questions as soon as there is evidence of a problem. Preparation can help. Ask yourself or some close advisors what the worst possible scenario may be. What is the best possible scenario? How will you react to either extreme? Are there other possible answers? Working through these questions and scenarios privately can remove the fear of the unknown because you have a prescribed, practiced reaction available to you.

Asking Questions Early

Questions focus our thinking. Ask empowering questions
like: What's good about this? What's not perfect about it
yet? What am I going to do next time? How can
I do this and have fun doing it?

CHARLES CONNOLLY
PSYCHOLOGIST

Make it a practice to notice the subtle changes and differences that are taking place within you and around you.

If you have an upset stomach, don't just swallow an over-the-counter remedy. Look for reasons why you are experiencing these symptoms. Is it what you've been eating? Is it stress? Is it eating too fast or too much? Is it the flu? The sooner you isolate the cause, the sooner you can address it. Treating the symptoms rarely takes care of the root cause.

If one of your colleagues or family members is acting differently toward you, resist the urge to take it personally and ask some questions. If you assume they are upset with you and avoid them or avoid looking into the reason for their behavior, a simple misunderstanding can snowball into a complete breakdown in communication.

Although we may fear the answers to our questions, by identifying the root cause of a situation, we can wisely use our time and energy to address it, rather than squandering it through fear, worry, and anxiety over an endless stream of possibilities.

Dogmatic Belief that What You "Know" Is True

Preconceived notions are the locks on the door to wisdom.

MERRY BROWNE
AUTHOR

We're trying to open up our perspective here. Analyzing where one of our beliefs comes from can allow us to see that there are other perspectives that could and should be considered. We don't have to actually use the ideas generated when considering the other perspectives. But expanding to see other viewpoints and asking questions about these viewpoints can increase curiosity, as illustrated by the following exercise.

1. Write down a statement that you "know" is true.
2. Answer the following questions:
   a. Why do I believe this is true?
   b. How do I know I'm right?
   c. If I'm wrong, what are some other possibilities? (List at least three.)
   d. How does this belief help me?
   e. How does this belief limit me?
3. Follow the "Curiosity Checklist" in Chapter 7 and investigate your belief. Play the role of "devil's advocate" and find as much evidence to challenge your belief as you can.

Fear of the Unknown

Not everything that is faced can be changed. But nothing can be changed until it is faced.

JAMES BALDWIN
AUTHOR

Fear of the unknown differs from the desire to avoid "what is" or "what may be" because with this barrier, we generally don't have any idea what's hiding in the dark or may be lurking around the next corner. The greater our imagination, the more vividly we can picture the monster under the bed. We can also imagine positive scenarios, like winning the lottery, getting a big raise, or being promoted.

Surprisingly, the stress of potentially hearing "good news" can be as intense as the stress of potential "bad news." In both scenarios, being curious and asking questions can result in getting answers that we don't feel we're ready or equipped to handle.

Reframe the unknown by acting as if you are a private investigator:

1. Take a few minutes to think about some of your favorite detectives from books, television shows, and movies.
2. Select your favorite and make a list of what you admire about him or her.
3. Choose a topic in the realm of the "unknown" that you are willing to investigate.
4. Emulate the character traits and behaviors of your favorite detective as you delve into the mystery you have chosen.

Insecurity or Feeling of Inadequacy

If you risk nothing, then you risk everything.

GEENA DAVIS
ACTRESS

It's frequently said that there are no dumb questions. I love to ask "dumb" questions. Let's replace the word "dumb" with the word "uninformed." There can be tremendous value in asking a question that no one else has asked. First of all, it is one of the most direct avenues to becoming informed. Second, many times, the question that you ask is one that others want to ask, but don't.

For the next week, ask one uninformed question per day. To be comfortable, it's OK to preface your question with something like, "This may be obvious, but. . . ."

Myth that an Answer or Better Approach Can't Be Found

What isn't tried won't work.

CLAUDE MCDONALD
PRESIDENT, INNOVATECH

Almost every problem has a variety of potential solutions, even if it looks as though no solutions exist. Often, when we are attempting to solve a problem that appears to be "unsolvable," our perspective that it will be difficult or impossible stops us from discovering the ways it might, in fact, be solved.

Asking the following questions will allow you to examine your basic premise, and view the problem from a broader perspective.

1. What, specifically, is the problem?
2. Why have people been unable to solve this problem thus far?
3. If the reasons in number two did not exist, how might the problem be solved?
4. What proof or theories are the answers given in number two based upon?
5. What, if any, conflicting evidence or theories currently exist?
6. What can we create that can eliminate or reduce the reasons given in number two?

Even if you don't manage to solve the "unsolvable," the exploration of the problem will produce experience and rich information that will probably be useful to you in the future.

The Value of Barriers

One of the secrets of life is to make stepping stones out of stumbling blocks.

JACK PENN
AUTHOR

Although we tend to think of barriers as "bad," they provide us with important information about who we are and how we function under various challenging conditions. As the proverb goes, "Smooth seas do not make skillful sailors." Every time we confront a barrier and find a way to remove it or go around it, we improve our problem-solving skills and the underlying curiosity muscles.

Rather than dreading the barriers that are certain to be ahead, try to anticipate them in the way an athlete looks forward to an upcoming race or game. Use your *Personal Brilliance Notebook* to keep a list of the barriers you overcome and reward yourself for your progress.

CHAPTER 10

Heightening CURIOSITY

The important thing is not to stop questioning. Curiosity has its own reason for existing.

ALBERT EINSTEIN
PHYSICIST

YOUR OUTCOMES are greatly determined by the quality of the questions that you ask yourself and others. Heightening your curiosity improves the quality of your life. People who are curious are open to thousands of potentialities and therefore increase their power to find the best solutions, the most lucrative offers, and the most creative ideas. Rather than being entrenched in their current beliefs, they withhold judgment, knowing that the last chapter has yet to be written.

AWARENESS
CURIOSITY
FOCUS
INITIATIVE

While the process of breaking curiosity barriers in the last chapter involved fortifying the weaker aspects, heightening curiosity is centered on uncovering and developing the inherent curiosity with which you were born.

The power that heightening your curiosity can create in your life is truly unlimited. When you put past judgments aside, you come up with some of your most innovative ideas.

What's at the Bottom of the Ocean?

The ocean depths remain one of the few unexplored areas of our planet. The scientists at the Monterey Bay Aquarium

Research Institute (MBARI) feel that the greatest discoveries in the science of oceans are still in our future. In the area of the Monterey Bay there are ocean canyons as deep as 4,000 meters in some spots. The question: What's down there?

Advances in remotely operated submersible vehicles have allowed exploration of these secret places to begin. First the curiosity, then the innovation required to begin to answer the question. Is this youthful curiosity about a new frontier enough to motivate scientists and financial backers like David Packard of Hewlett Packard fame to pursue the risks involved in deep-sea exploration? The questions generated by a heightened sense of curiosity get the process rolling. Practical innovations—results—keep the questions coming.

Mario Tamburri, a marine ecologist at MBARI, was curious about the problem of foreign aquatic species being introduced to coastal waters outside of their normal region. This foreign marine life can cause enormous damage to the ecology of the native community where the species land. This problem is thought to have caused approximately 70 percent of native aquatic species extinctions in the last 100 years.

How do these foreign species travel? Previous studies have shown that the water in the ballast tanks of ships inadvertently transports these organisms. Many different approaches to solve this problem proved too expensive. One solution that held the most promise was de-oxygenation, which is the process of bubbling nitrogen into the ballast tanks, removing the oxygen, and thereby safely and effectively killing the majority of the organisms found in the ballast. But de-oxygenation also proved expensive, and so shipping companies wouldn't voluntarily use the process.

Tamburri answered another question: What will make this workable process a viable approach?

"De-oxygenation was seen as too expensive for controlling invasive species in ballast water, but our study shows that the anticorrosion benefit of this technique is a strong economic incentive for the shipping industry," said Tamburri. "It's a win-win treatment for solving an environmental problem and reducing ship maintenance costs." It is estimated that nearly US $100,000 per year can be saved for each new ship that uses this de-oxygenation technique instead of painting to prevent rust.

Because of heightened curiosity MBARI created an innovative, environmentally benign solution to multiple problems, while also saving ship owners money through rust prevention. Personal brilliance at work.

Techniques to Heighten Your Curiosity

Try New Things

Discoveries are often made by not following instructions,
by going off the main road, by trying the untried.

FRANK TYGER
FORBES MAGAZINE

Take a class. Research a new area that you would like to learn more about. Take up a new mini-hobby. Taste a food that is new to you. See a movie that you normally wouldn't be attracted to. Read a book on a topic that is unfamiliar. When you try new things and are in learning mode, you ask questions. The more you put yourself in learning and questioning mode, the more you develop curiosity as a habit.

Seek Out Experts

When we are confronted with problems,
the counsel of someone who has mastered similar
problems can be a great help.

PATANJALI
INDIAN YOGI AND AUTHOR OF *PATANJALI'E YOGASUTRAS*

Seek out experts on the subject. Many times a quick call to someone who has experience with a similar problem can make the difference. Don't be intimidated by the expert status. Your curiosity is often the key to obtaining access. Experts often enjoy sharing their knowledge. You see, these experts also possess a heightened level of curiosity and will tend to recognize you as a kindred spirit. Ask, and you shall receive.

Conduct Research

> *The best effect of any book is that it excites*
> *the reader to self-activity.*
>
> THOMAS CARLYLE
> SCOTTISH PHILOSOPHER AND AUTHOR

Brilliance is difficult to delegate. Although you frequently can benefit from research gathered by others, you can also miss a great deal if you don't conduct research for yourself. Curiosity feeds itself. One question leads to another, based on your filters in solving the problem. So, do your own research wherever possible and ask your own questions.

Seek Alternative Solutions

> *Go the extra mile. It's never crowded.*
>
> EXECUTIVE SPEECHWRITER NEWSLETTER

So, you've identified a workable solution. A possible innovation. If at all possible, extend your curiosity to explore some possible alternative solutions. This will help when you're selling your idea and also provide a fallback approach if the original idea breaks down in some way.

In the book, *If It Ain't Broke . . . Break It!*, authors Robert

Kriegel and Louis Patler make the argument that there is no such thing as a finished product. Becoming complacent regarding an innovation in a changing world is the first step to extinction.

As an exercise to heighten curiosity regarding a working solution, ask how it could be done differently. Although this is an exercise, you may identify a new approach that can lead to a significant innovation.

Seek Non-Experts' Opinions

Even when the experts all agree, they may well be mistaken.

BERTRAND RUSSELL
THE SKEPTICAL ESSAYS

As mentioned above, you can benefit from seeking out experts in a particular field. But, interestingly, people who have little or no experience with the subject you are exploring can be the most refreshing sources of new information. These sources are not entrenched in assumptions and mindsets because they lack experience in the given area.

Brilliance is often about perspective. There are numerous examples of brilliant solutions coming by accident as the innovator works on something else. To increase the possibilities for brilliance, you need to increase your perspective. Expanding your perspective through other people's ideas can heighten your curiosity. Seeking the opinions of people who have little experience with the problem may provide the added perspective you need for a breakthrough. For any new idea, seek opinions from those outside your area of expertise. In between plays at your child's ball game, ask a fellow parent how they might improve upon your latest idea. Or ask a question like, "If your profession was X, would you buy this product?"

The people closest to you can be very valuable resources. They know you well—both your strengths and your weaknesses. Many times, though, they don't know you in a work environment. Friends and family members can often recognize how you can apply your strengths to a work situation in a way that may not be obvious to you because you're mired in the details. Frequently, they can offer a practical perspective that you may be overlooking.

Ask for opinions. Who knows where that great idea may come from?

Don't Compartmentalize Your Life

Another way to heighten curiosity is to move beyond the concept of compartmentalizing your life in an attempt to achieve "balance." (Compartmentalization is discussed further in Chapter 13.)

One of the biggest downsides of compartmentalization as a way to achieve life balance is the isolation it creates. When one compartment of your life is preventing access to another compartment, there is an internal communication breakdown. Perhaps the activities in your home and family compartment could contribute to brilliant solutions in your sports compartment. Another drawback is the opportunity cost of being unable to seek ideas from potentially valuable resources.

The concept of compartmentalization is best understood if we analyze the often-heard phrase, "Leave your work at the office." Many life balance experts suggest that we attempt to leave our problems, and therefore our stress, at the office and seek a buffer zone to de-stress as we leave our professional life and move into our personal life. Unfortunately, many

CEOs we work with in our executive advisory practice are highly schooled in this skill.

It makes sense that if you're upset at work it's not a good idea to come home and kick the dog, yell at the kids, and grumble at your spouse. However, by being unwilling to share some of your work-related problems at home, you miss out on the input of very important advisors. It is possible to share a problem without dumping your anger and frustration on the person you're sharing it with. A side benefit is the teaching opportunity your situation may provide to those close to you.

Work Like a Detective

> *Problems cannot be solved at the same level*
> *of awareness that created them.*
>
> ALBERT EINSTEIN
> PHYSICIST

Good detectives follow all potential leads, often gathering a huge amount of possibly relevant information, much of which turns out to be useless. However, their attention to detail can eventually pan out when they find the one thread that leads them to a solution.

The infamous Son of Sam murderer in New York was apprehended by very detailed detective work. Ultimately his downfall was a parking ticket he received while parked in the neighborhood of one of the murders. A detective team painstakingly searched through the large volume of detail necessary to solve the problem. They didn't know if it would pan out until it did, but they still went through the process. Ask questions. Look at everything. Follow every lead.

Notice and Eliminate Assumptions

If you would be a real seeker of truth, it's necessary that, at least once in your life you doubt, as far as possible, all things.

RENÉ DESCARTES
FRENCH PHILOSOPHER AND SCIENTIST

Questions come in layers. We can only keep so much straight in our minds, so we revert to assumptions to help move to the next question. This helps us keep all the data organized, but be careful not to believe the assumptions. Don't forget to go back and challenge the existing belief. Perhaps the answer is hidden by a "faulty fact." This is where healthy doubt can be very productive.

Fire Your Inner Critic

*Any fool can criticize, condemn, and complain—
and most fools do.*

DALE CARNEGIE
AUTHOR AND TRAINER

Someone must have thought of this before.

There are lots of smart people out there.

I couldn't possibly have come up with something unique.

These are the kinds of thoughts that can kill an innovation before it's born. Remember that someone had every great idea in history. Why not you? We can be so critical of ourselves. Fire that inner critic. Later in the innovation process there will be plenty of nay-sayers.

Give your ideas time to develop. Respect your intuition. Let ideas percolate for a time prior to applying a critical eye.

The ideas will either develop to fruition or their pitfalls will emerge. The key is to give them a chance.

"Browse" Everywhere

Curiosity is the thirst of the soul.

SAMUEL JOHNSON
THE RAMBLER

Browse at the newsstand. What new magazines are out there? Why does this newsstand carry the titles that it does? What is it about the traffic pattern and clientele that dictates the offerings? How could one of the papers or books that you might normally not purchase help you with something you're working on?

Browse at the library. The card catalog is great, but I've found that the really valuable nuggets are buried in a paragraph on a page of a book that I would never have discovered by searching for titles. This may sound strange, but I frequently walk up and down the aisles in the library seeing if a particular book "calls" to me from the shelf. Free your curiosity.

Browse at friends' homes. Of course, stick with what's in the open! Why have they decorated their home the way they have? Does the layout fit the personality of your friend as you have interpreted it? What questions can you ask based on what you've browsed that will allow you to learn more about your friend and deepen the relationship?

Browse the Yellow Pages. The number of seemingly strange businesses is truly amazing. Browse the Yellow Pages and ask, why? Some example categories that caught my attention in the past include:

- Abattoirs
- Barbershop equipment
- Change-making machines
- Erosion control
- Glass circles and other special shapes
- Hub caps
- Pet cemeteries
- Popcorn supplies
- Pony rides
- Ultra-light aircraft

Explore New Places and Types of Information

The value of experience is not in seeing much,
but in seeing wisely.

Sir William Osler
Canadian physician

Routine is so comfortable and certainly serves a purpose. However, the next time you have a chance to see someplace new, take advantage of the opportunity. Consider checking out a new restaurant, or taking a weekend car trip to attend a sporting event or play. While exploring, ask as many questions as possible. Think of one or two people who would love to hear about your discoveries, and then listen and observe well enough so that you can tell them what you learned when you return. This focused curiosity will help increase your awareness as you explore as well.

How do you get your information? Business travelers are very familiar with *USA Today*. If you're more used to your local paper, every once in a while pick up a *USA Today* and compare the different approaches to providing the news. Try different TV shows. Try a new search engine on the Internet.

Periodically, change your filter for information and you may find the different perspective that can lead to an innovation.

Vary Your Daily Routine

It is easier to behave your way into a new way of thinking than to think your way into a new way of behaving.

KEGLEY'S "PRINCIPLE OF CHANGE"
FROM JOHN PEERS, *1,001 LOGICAL LAWS*

Take different routes to work, or school, or the market. Use your curiosity to see how many ways you can get there from here. Ask directions of a number of people and evaluate how many variations you hear in these directions. Try them all and evaluate the differences. Use your *Personal Brilliance Notebook* to record your observations. Record the practical aspects of the directions and routes. Also record your reaction to those providing directions. What was their attitude? Did their perspective change as they began providing information?

Ask More Questions

Learning is not attained by chance. It must be sought for with ardor and attended to with diligence.

ABIGAIL ADAMS
U.S. FIRST LADY

When you meet new people, find out what they do. Most people have a pretty standard answer to this mundane question, usually relating to the work they do or the main focus of their lives. The more interesting question is, "What else do you do?" This question usually takes people off guard and jolts them into a more reflective mode in which they tend to reveal their passions—their family, their hobbies, and their goals.

Find out how their interest began, and how these activities fit into the world. This is much more interesting and you learn so much more.

*   *   *

When you develop heightened curiosity, you improve the quality of your life by asking quality questions and being receptive to trying on new ideas. Heighten your curiosity by training the curiosity muscles regularly.

The following list is a recap of the techniques you can use to heighten your curiosity.

Intensify Your Curiosity

- Try new things. Even if they don't work out, you'll learn lessons to apply elsewhere.
- Seek out experts for their views.
- Do your own research.
- Seek alternative solutions, even when all is well. This gives you fallback positions.
- Routinely seek opinions from people who have no experience with the subject.
- Don't compartmentalize your life. This creates artificial barriers to brilliant solutions.
- When you have a problem, work like a detective. Ask questions. Look at everything. Follow every lead.
- Notice and eliminate assumptions. They're usually wrong.
- Fire your inner critic. Give ideas time to percolate before assessing them.
- "Browse" everywhere.
- Explore new places and types of information.
- Take different routes in your daily routine.
- Ask questions of those you encounter: Find out what they do and what else they do.

SECTION IV

FOCUS

CHAPTER 11

The Power of FOCUS

> No horse gets anywhere until he is
> harnessed. No stream or gas drives anything
> until it is confined. No Niagara is ever turned
> into light and power until it is tunneled. No
> life ever grows great until it is focused,
> dedicated, disciplined.
>
> HARRY EMERSON FOSDICK
> MINISTER

AWARENESS and curiosity, two of the catalysts of innovation, expand your options, but to move toward a solution, you need to focus—to go beneath the surface and give full attention to what you're doing.

On the surface, awareness and focus may seem to contradict each other. If we're aware of as much as possible, aren't we indeed un-focused? Our awareness exercises are designed to help us experience more and more. In today's information society, aren't we getting too much data? Focus sounds like just what we need to cut through all the miscellaneous information and get down to what matters. Let's be careful. Focus is not about exclusion or minimizing our inputs.

Focus with a 360-Degree View

*In a narrow circle the mind grows narrow. The more one
expands, the larger their aims.*

JOHANN FRIEDRICH VON SCHILLER
GERMAN DRAMATIST, POET, AND HISTORIAN

Expanding your focus is one of the most helpful aspects of developing personal brilliance. When I talk about focus, I'm not referring to a laser beam type of perspective, where you block out everything but the opportunity or problem at hand. Instead, when I say focus, I am referring to a 360-degree view. This type of focus is more like a broad spotlight that expands in a circle around an issue rather than a pinpointed laser. Focusing like a spotlight allows us to be aware of all that is within this wide circle of light. When you expand your focus, you avoid becoming myopic and create a bigger sphere in which to operate.

Solving the Focus Paradox

*Soft focus is an important skill that can affect us
metaphorically. In other words, the way we see the future
has everything to do with how well we can look up and see
the expanded horizon before us.*

PETER KLINE
"PEAK PERFORMANCE" EXPERT

Focusing like a spotlight means going beneath the surface and giving full attention to what you're doing, without excluding ideas that are on the periphery of your awareness. Remember that in our discussion of black-and-white thinking in the Awareness section, we said that the opportunity is often in the gray area. It's important that you don't exclude important information from the equation because that is where the opportunity usually lies. Our first paradox: Although we want a greater focus, we also want the focus to be more open than restrictive.

A great example of this paradox occurred with a researcher in our office. After identifying the specific components for an article we were writing on the subject of focus, she started with Web searches on key words like attention, concentration, and procrastination. She was laser-beam focused on her task. However, she was frustrated with the volume of general results. Only after stepping back a bit and realizing that she needed to expand her target to search for more global terms including the most obvious one—"how to focus"—was she able to find a great deal of specific information.

Regardless of the task, focus pays. In *Finding Flow*, Mihaly Csikszentmihalyi explains that people feel the worst—worse than when they are forced to do things—when they act by default and without focus.

Focus is related to awareness in that focus is about the present. It's about *now*. In effect, every step of the process should be thought of as having a beginning, middle, and end in itself, with complete attention given to each activity in the process until that activity is completed.

Focus is completely based in the present—when what you are doing is the same as what you are thinking. When you are in a focused state there is a feeling of mental smoothness. A lot is happening, but it's not jerky. This is not to say that there isn't intensity in your brain activity but it tends to be productive. It's virtually impossible to force great performance through thought or analysis. With the right focus you don't become overly analytical.

When you're in the present, you move to the involuntary type of focus you're seeking for peak performance. It's an automatic feeling. The mind is in a zone of focus that produces smooth activity and results.

The main reason many of my coaching clients struggle is a lack of focus. Procrastination sets in with the resulting negative cycle of guilt and fear. This is not a confident position. This lack of confidence translates into more fear causing further paralysis. At some point in this cycle the client seeks some sort of organizational program—"If only I could be more organized."

Unfortunately brute force doesn't work well. A second paradox: Sometimes we need to stop trying to focus on an issue for a period of time in order to be able to focus better.

A sports analogy is a great way to explain this. In tennis, for example, studies have shown that the ball is actually in play only 20 percent of the match. The remaining 80 percent of the time is downtime: time spent on breaks, walking around between points, and getting ready. Total focus is necessary during the 20 percent of uptime—no interruptions, no thoughts of other areas of your life. However, it's not possible to keep up this level of focus for extended periods of time. Even athletes in the "zone" talk of a ratcheting up of focus for the uptime portion of the sport. They have to switch in and out, focusing exclusively on the ball during uptime and then relaxing the focus during the downtime. This takes a great deal of practice for the athlete in a pressure-packed situation. We'll borrow from this type of sports-based training to develop our focus via exercises in upcoming chapters.

It's easy to focus on something if you enjoy it. Have you ever been lost in a great movie or a book? The feeling is that time is suspended and you are surprised how connected you are with the material. Concentration on the material comes easily. If someone walks in the room you may not even notice. This level of focus flows naturally and easily. Have you ever witnessed someone practice a complex craft or artistic technique in which they spend hours focused on their seemingly tedious task? A great short-order cook is like an air traffic controller of the kitchen, coordinating multiple meals at various states of preparation. It's a thing of beauty. How do they do it? Do you have an area in your own life where focus comes easily, involuntarily?

Professional athletes have the ability to "make it look easy." This is a result of mastery. This is rarely true in Little League, though we see that the game obviously comes more easily for some players than others. Perhaps the shortstop always knows the overall status of the game while the second baseman doesn't even realize a ground ball was hit in his area? Although there could be many physiological and other reasons for the second baseman's lack of focus (I struck out regularly until I discovered I needed glasses), with all things being equal, the shortstop may just have a greater interest in the game.

Find Your Game

There has never been another you. With no effort on your part you were born to be something very special and set apart. What you are going to do in appreciation of that gift is a decision only you can make.

DAN ZADRA
AUTHOR

The first step is to choose your game wisely. This applies to both your personal life and your professional life. Stack the deck. If you're doing something that you love and that is naturally interesting, then involuntary focus happens easily. It's all right to wander a bit to determine what your perfect situation is. Don't beat yourself up if you're still in search mode. Learn from those experiences, place them in the past, and count them as a part of your journey.

Even if you love what you're doing, sometimes focus is difficult. It is difficult to force yourself to perform in any activity without preparation. If you haven't jogged or briskly walked in twenty years, it's not likely that you will successfully complete a marathon tomorrow. Some training is necessary. The same is true for your focus muscles.

Focus can really pay off, but it may take some diligence. Howard Schultz, raised in a Brooklyn, New York, housing project, can identify the pivot point in his life when he visited a coffee-bean store in Seattle called Starbucks. It took a year to convince the Starbucks owners to hire him as director of marketing and operations. His awareness came into play while traveling in Italy. He noticed that the espresso bars served as meeting places that were a significant part of the culture.

When Schultz tried to promote this concept at the coffee-bean store back in Seattle, he encountered resistance. The owners simply didn't want to get into the restaurant business. Frustrated, Schultz left to start his own coffee bar business but never lost his focus, buying Starbucks a year later. This focus caused Starbucks to become a household name throughout the country and the world.

What if you are faced with some aspects of your life where focus does not come easily? Some portions of what you do may be more difficult than others. For example, you may be great at doing presentations for your job but not be as comfortable communicating in written form. How do you simulate the easy flow of involuntary focus when you want it to kick in?

Fake It!

Men acquire a particular quality by constantly acting a particular way . . . you become just by performing just actions, temperate by performing temperate actions, brave by performing brave actions.

ARISTOTLE
GREEK PHILOSOPHER

Fake it. That's right. Fake it! When you experience involuntary focus it's magical, right? There's no conscious effort on your part. You're in the flow. Why? You're into it. You are excited about it. You're interested in what you're doing. This overcomes the effort you must expend. You don't even realize you're working, either mentally or physically. You see a purpose to your action. It may simply be learning. Or it may be that you know how you will use the result of your work.

Let me give you an example. I have not proven to be great at wrapping presents. Most definitely someone else who is better qualified should perform this task for me. However, this past holiday I decided to wrap my wife's gift. It was a huge box. Traditional wrapping paper wouldn't work. Aha, an idea. I will create my own wrapping paper with a personalized message. Now, the benefit of this idea is that my wife knows that someone else always wraps her gifts. She would get a laugh and hopefully also think I was cute. So I repeated the words Merry Christmas over and over in a fancy font and printed fifty copies of the sheet on the color printer. Then I taped these individual pieces of paper all over the box.

Trust me, in the traditional sense this wasn't necessarily the best use of my time. And certainly I categorize gift-wrapping as something I don't do. But, I had a blast. I enjoyed every minute of it. Why? I could easily see the purpose in what I was doing. It was a small personal act for the woman I love. I visualized her reaction when she saw the package. I made it fun and child-like.

Another task that tests focus for me is the creation of my monthly e-mail newsletter on the subject of leading organizational change. Although it can be a bit tedious, there is a process, which helps. I know that the most productive mental state to be in is when I can clearly see the thousands of subscribers looking forward to receiving the *ADVISORY*, eager for the latest information. I know that some organizations use the newsletter as a basis for their staff meeting discussions. So, when that mood strikes, when I'm really jazzed about the subject matter, I ride the wave of focus. In this state I have written enough content for six issues in one sitting (approximately 12,000 words).

Keep your purpose in front of you. What is the outcome you desire from the activity? How can you make it fun? How can you link what you love with the activity that doesn't interest you?

Payoffs of Focus

I feel that the most important step in any major accomplishment is setting a specific goal. This enables you to keep your mind focused on your goal and off the many obstacles that will arise when you're striving to do your best.

KURT THOMAS
GYMNAST

With finely tuned focus, a number of benefits are available:

- Because of the focus applied to tasks, there is a tendency to do things right the first time, reducing the duration of the task and ultimately saving time.

- More goals are achieved with a focused mind set.
- As more goals are achieved, confidence improves.
- With confidence, peace of mind is enhanced.
- Smooth focus provides a control that improves all aspects of life.

In the next chapter, we will explore attention and concentration and their relation to focus.

CHAPTER 12

Attention, Rhythm, and PURPOSE

When we talk about understanding, surely it takes place only when the mind listens completely—the mind being your heart, your nerves, your ears—when you give your whole attention to it."

JIDDU KRISHNAMURTI
INDIAN THEOSOPHIST

TO USE a computer analogy for our brain, the ability to pay *attention* and concentrate on a task is like the random access memory (RAM) in your computer. In a computer, when RAM is full, no other processing can occur. So, our attention span is the length of time we can concentrate on an activity or an idea. By expanding the amount of available RAM the computer can accomplish a great deal more. The same is true for our ability to accomplish more with our mental and physical tools.

AWARENESS
CURIOSITY
FOCUS
INITIATIVE

Concentration is what allows the mind and body to move toward the achievement of a goal. Concentration is a focusing of your thoughts, feelings, and efforts. Concentration is the trigger that engages the brain to process the data through a filtering system that allows it to be categorized for use so it can be retained and recalled. Basically, concentration is required for memory. If you are focused during an event there is a greater likelihood that you will better re-member the event in the future.

Concentration involves being attentive to a wide range of data coming from all of your senses as it passes through your mind. Your ability to absorb everything that comes at you in the richest detail has a direct relationship to your ability to later recall and use the information. Remembering is a pro-cess of recalling a string of data in a particular order. That is only possible if the information is filed in a logical way. That is the *purpose* of concentration and focus.

Rhythm Starts with a Ritual

If we were to ask the brain how it would like to be treated, whether shaken at a random, irregular rate, or in a rhythmic, harmonious fashion, we can be sure that the brain, or for that matter the whole body, would prefer the latter.

ITZHAK BENTOV
STALKING THE WILD PENDULUM

There is a rhythm to proper focus. We're searching for a smooth flow that allows a successful performance, whether we're shooting a basketball or analyzing how to engage a teen-ager in their studies. Rhythm starts with a ritual that triggers our focus. The skilled golfer uses a pre-shot ritual or routine that is employed every time, the same way. There is a rhythm to the pre-shot routine, a cadence that is repeatable.

This is the answer to being able to turn the switch on when you need it. As we discussed earlier, it's not feasible to maintain a high degree of focus for an extended period of time. The ritual used during downtime is just as important. You can easily lose the focus state during pauses in the action. So, a ritual that allows you to maintain your rhythm while in a resting state is critical.

For instance, when I'm attending a business meeting, my pre-meeting routine involves taking out my notebook and noting the meeting title and date. While this may seem like a simple act, for me, this trigger brings up the proper level of focus. I have attended thousands of business meetings and have used that practice to link the proper level of focus that is effective for me to the trigger. Your trigger may be different.

During breaks in the meeting I rest my brain but I want to maintain the rhythm. I usually strike up a conversation with one of the participants on a current event or something in their lives. I'm looking to exercise my awareness, curiosity, and focus at a low level, so when the meeting resumes I can easily shift back up to a higher focus level.

My triggers are slightly different when I'm speaking to an audience. The energy has to be just right. Again, I know from experience how I should feel before going on stage to be successful, and I get into that rhythm. A conversation with my wife requires a different level of clarity and focus. Getting into the proper state is crucial for success in the varied interactions we have throughout the day.

Seeking the Greater Purpose

Clarity is the counterbalance of profound thoughts.

MARQUIS DE VAUVENARGUES
FRENCH MORALIST

There must be a purpose to justify and motivate our focus. It's important to move from a state of "have to" to a state of "want to" in regard to any task. For example, in one of my professional associations (National Speakers Association) I listen to a large number of professional speakers addressing a variety of topics. Some of these speeches cover topics I am very interested in, while the content of others holds little, if any, interest. Also, some of the speakers are brilliant and some are still learning and honing their skills.

If my purpose was solely my own enlightenment and entertainment based on the content and performance of the speaker, I would walk out of many of these sessions or at least fall asleep. However, my purpose extends beyond the session. I'm looking below the surface for why and how they are doing what they do. Many times I learn much more from the novices than I do from the masters. The greater purpose keeps me engaged and focused in these presentations. I ensure that I receive something valuable from every presentation I attend.

Can you find a greater purpose for the activities you are required to participate in but that may not, at least on the surface, be on the top of your interest list?

Clarity should be a goal in regard to purpose. With awareness, curiosity, and focus, developing a habit for seeking a clear picture of what you are engaged with will allow you to perform at a new level. A crystal-clear picture of your personal plan and what you want to achieve is necessary to allow focus to flow. This clear picture allows you to place your activities into a context.

Focus on Clear, Yet Flexible, Goals

Your plan should be balanced across all aspects of your life. Choose the categories that are most appropriate for you, but here are six (in no particular order) that apply to most people:

• *Health and Fitness.* This category encompasses your nutrition, exercise, and health risk prevention activities. Don't forget that gathering health knowledge is necessary to keep up with the latest theories on great health.

- *Business/Career.* These goals may include specifics such as sales targets as well as broader goals, such as education and growth requirements.
- *Relationships/Family.* What habits should be created to enhance your relationships? Identify which relationships are most important and how you will bolster them for the long term.
- *Financial.* Your plan should include total income, the money you want to save and invest, and if necessary, the amount of debt to be eliminated.
- *Spiritual/Emotional.* The plan in this area relates to the foundation and internal infrastructure that contribute to your peace of mind and inner strength.
- *Contribution.* This area of your plan defines what you do to contribute to your community. Remember that contributions can take many forms, not just monetary.

As you build the goals in each area of your life, be careful to ensure that each goal is outcome based. First, what is your purpose? What is the outcome you are trying to achieve? What actions, if completed successfully, will guarantee that outcome? This approach allows flexibility in your planning. A plan that is too rigid can actually preclude innovation. If you're laser-beam focused on your "to do" list at the expense of seeing what is happening around you, you may be able to check items off the list and not meet your desired outcome. This doesn't mean that we bounce from one idea to another. Flexibility in the plan, within the context of your purpose, provides guidance while allowing you to fully take advantage of the right opportunities.

Have you had an experience where all the tasks were completed but the outcome was not reached? In contrast, think about a time you failed to execute your plan but still reached the desired outcome because you had a clear sense of purpose regarding the outcome and results you wanted. Your purpose needs to be your own purpose, not someone else's.

I know a man whose belief system said that to be a good provider for his family he had to have some sort of management job, work in an office, and wear a suit and tie to work. However, his greatest talent was working with his hands. He loved to garden, to care for animals, and was brilliant with a piece of wood. Only after he retired from a frustrating and mediocre career did he allow himself to pursue his dream of furniture restoration. What innovation was missed because of this mismatch created merely because his own purpose was set aside?

Calculating Opportunity Cost

The cost of a thing is the amount of what I will call life which is required to be exchanged for it, immediately or in the long run.

HENRY DAVID THOREAU
ESSAYIST, POET, AND NATURALIST

Opportunity cost is a term used regularly in economics. The concept of opportunity cost is that the true cost of something is what you must give up to get it. For example, if a student is tabulating the cost of a law school education, she must consider not only the cost of tuition, books, and other educational expenses, but also the loss of salary she could earn during those three years. Now, if you also consider that she is giving up the ability to train in some other arena during this time you can see that the hidden opportunity costs can be significant.

The cost of going to the movies isn't simply the cost of tickets and the extraordinary price of popcorn, but also what you may have earned if you were working toward a goal during those two hours. Of course, this cost is justified if going to the movies serves one of your other goals. Purpose is what's important.

The phrase, "I work better under pressure" in relation to concentration is true to an extent. The deadline pressure may create the temporary purpose needed to get the job done. However, what is the opportunity cost? How much better would the solution be if the task was performed in a more methodical way?

Recognizing Patterns

You have to see the pattern, understand the order and experience the vision.

MICHAEL E. GERBER
BUSINESSMAN, CONSULTANT, AND AUTHOR

How can you function in a world that is so complex? You encounter so much that is new each day. How do you possibly grasp what is happening in this ever-changing environment? Our brains are capable of pattern recognition. You can recognize a pattern, then apply context to the pattern and determine meaning. For example, if you see a vertical line with a horizontal line intersecting it approximately one quarter of the way from the top, you can identify what you are seeing. Depending on the context, it could either be a cross used as a religious symbol or it may be the letter "t."

Granted, you have to have been exposed to the alphabet. But the beauty of pattern recognition is that you could still recognize and assign meaning to the "t" whether or not you ever saw the word it was used in. In fact your knowledge of the letter "t" could help you identify the brand-new word.

In this example you also have to have been exposed to a cross as a religious symbol. Your ability to focus helps build the context in the computer that is your mind. Your experiences will help you distinguish between a crucifix, an ornate Orthodox cross, or a burning cross on a lawn. Moving through life with focus helps make these distinctions, giving greater depth to our understanding. Innovation can spring from this type of detailed observation.

Experts who create great value are masters at using their power of focus to recognize patterns that the uninitiated miss. A political analyst, for example, can notice the slight nuance in a politician's pattern of speech that indicates a change in policy. A mother can identify the minute shift in an eyebrow that says her daughter is not feeling well. This type of expertise is developed via a strong level of purpose, interest, and finely tuned focusing skills.

Create a Trigger

*It's not the will to win, but the will to prepare
to win that makes the difference.*

PAUL "BEAR" BRYANT
FOOTBALL COACH

We don't live in a laboratory. Things are moving quickly. You need to be able to focus fast, pay attention with the proper concentration, and deal with more and more distractions. The mind works with the body. The best way to let your mind know that it's time to focus is with a trigger mechanism. Select a word or physical gesture that can serve as your trigger. In a state of relaxation, conjure up what it feels like to be acutely aware. Relax your eyes. Take in all that you can see. Listen intently. Notice the texture of what is under your hand. Identify the scents in the air. Crystallize your focus.

Now, while in this state of focus execute your trigger mechanism repeatedly in order to groove the connection between the trigger mechanism and your state of focus. This trigger mechanism is very powerful. Think of the effect of the lights going down in a movie theater. We have trained ourselves that it's time to focus on the screen rather than the comfort of our seat or situating our popcorn and drink. When the lights go down, you know what to do. With practice, your chosen trigger mechanism can automatically tell you what to do.

CHAPTER 13

Breaking Through Focus
BARRIERS

As long as a man stands in his own way,
everything seems to be in his way.
RALPH WALDO EMERSON
WRITER AND PHILOSOPHER

WE ALL have barriers that block our expanded focus. Some
of these barriers are internal, such as anxieties, boredom, and
hundreds of different thoughts that take our attention off on
tangents. Other focus barriers are external. They include the
people or circumstances that you can't seem to "see beyond."

One of the most exciting things about breaking through
focus barriers is seeing farther than you've
ever seen before. You not only notice more,
you begin to see how all of your knowledge
and experience is interlinked; how everything
in your 360-degree world is a resource for creating innovative projects, hurdling challenges,
and solving problems. When you break through focus barriers, your entire world opens up and personal brilliance shines
through.

AWARENESS
CURIOSITY
FOCUS
INITIATIVE

This process begins with a self-assessment of your most
dominant focus blocks. Once you determine these blocks, you
can break through them by practicing the strategies discussed
later in the chapter.

Focus Barriers and Descriptions

To identify your dominant focus barriers, read the brief descriptions that follow the list of six barriers, and then note those barriers that apply to you. Once you've determined your biggest blocks, begin using the strategies provided and break through to expanded focus!

___Activities that don't interest you
___Self-consciousness
___Life balance
___A narrow focus
___Interruptions
___Physiology

Activities that Don't Interest You

Sometimes only a change of viewpoint is needed to convert a tiresome duty into an interesting opportunity.

ALBERTA FLANDERS
AUTHOR

Have you ever noticed that when you're doing something you enjoy, you're right there in the moment? Your mind is on what you're doing, and you're awake and alert. On the other hand, when you're doing something like filing a week's worth of memos, or ironing clothes, your mind continually wanders away from the task. While there's a lot to be said for daydreaming, if you're not focusing on what is happening here and now, you're missing a lot. If you find your mind wandering frequently during disliked tasks, this is a focus barrier well worth breaking through.

Self-Consciousness

Inspiration may be a form of superconsciousness, or perhaps of subconsciousness—I wouldn't know. But I am sure it is the antithesis of self-consciousness.

AARON COPLAND
COMPOSER

Self-awareness, as we learned, is an important part of our habit of personal brilliance. *Self-consciousness*, however, is a barrier we need to avoid. Self-consciousness acts as a governor on our actions, which causes us to hold back. If you are concerned, to the point of distraction, about how you will be perceived, your focus suffers. Self-consciousness has to do with something that may happen in the future (how you are perceived) and focus requires being in the present.

Life Balance

Just as your car runs more smoothly and requires less energy to go faster and farther when the wheels are in perfect alignment, you perform better when your thoughts, feelings, emotions, goals, and values are in balance.

BRIAN TRACY
TRAINER, SPEAKER, AUTHOR, AND BUSINESSMAN

When thinking about focus, it's easy to conjure up thoughts of Thomas Edison sleeping in his laboratory. Or, from more recent memory, how about the engineers from Apple Computer, not sleeping for four days straight, living on pizza and Coke? Boy, that really sounds glamorous and exciting, doesn't it? Sure, as long as someone else is doing it. But you or I might say, "I don't want to be a workaholic" or "I can't be innovative, I have a family. I want to have balance."

The pursuit of balance today is very important. Two thirds (66 percent) of American workers and three quarters (77 percent) of British workers list their number one cause of stress as too heavy of a workload. "I don't have time to be innovative!" However, maintaining balance in your life does not mean that you should seek to compartmentalize each area of your life. In fact, true life balance requires just the opposite—a seamless blending of all aspects of your life into one complete whole.

A Narrow Focus

All of us are watchers—of television, of time clocks,
of traffic on the freeway—but few are observers.
Everyone is looking, not many are seeing.

PETER M. LESCHAK
AUTHOR

As we discussed in Chapter 11, focus should be an open process. Too narrow a focus may create blind spots that preclude seeing all the possibilities available. The illusionist counts on your very narrow focus and attention in order to pull off his "magic" tricks. If focus is too narrow, important pieces of information may be missed. A tight focus is usually most beneficial as a release or a break, such as when teenagers are fully absorbed in their Gameboy, but this type of focus can be limiting when trying to get something accomplished.

Interruptions

The average American worker has fifty interruptions a day,
of which 70 percent have nothing to do with work.

W. EDWARDS DEMING
MANAGEMENT CONSULTANT

Interruptions will happen. The rest of the world is not necessarily on our schedule. If we're not properly focused on an activity, it is difficult to get back to it after an interruption. How do you handle interruptions? Think back to times when you were interrupted over the last week. Were the interruptions pleasant or unpleasant? Were you able to easily return to the task? Did the interruption create new tasks? What was the most valuable interruption to you during this period?

Physiology

> All this sensory input, which begins in the brain,
> has its effect throughout the body.
>
> NORMAN COUSINS
> EDITOR, HUMANITARIAN, AND AUTHOR

Physical fitness is a key component in focus. You will frequently hear golfers credit their improved fitness program for allowing them to better focus at the end of their round. Nutrition plays a big part in our ability to focus. Caffeine, processed sugars, and flours, and food allergies can all have a negative impact on focus.

Even temporary, modest hypoglycemia (low blood sugar) slows down our ability to process visual and auditory information and causes us to have more difficulty concentrating. Do you feel tired and sluggish mid-afternoon? When you're hungry, does that become your dominant thought, impeding your focus?

Strategies for Breaking Through Focus Barriers

Activities that Don't Interest You

> Today is life—the only life you are sure of. Make the most of today. Get interested in something. Shake yourself awake.

Develop a hobby. Let the winds of enthusiasm sweep through you. Live today with gusto.

DALE CARNEGIE
AUTHOR AND TRAINER

One way to expand your focus when you're engaged in a task that doesn't interest you is to find out how it's connected to something that you do find interesting.

For example, let's say that one of your responsibilities is to rake the autumn leaves, but this is a task that's anything but interesting to you. Ask yourself, what is associated with raking leaves that I *do* find interesting? Perhaps you enjoy hearing the birds sing, or love the way the air smells so fresh and crisp? Is this a time for you to get a little exercise, or observe what's happening in your neighborhood?

By linking this "uninteresting" chore to things that you value, you open your focus to the moment and break through this barrier.

Self-Consciousness

Sensitiveness is closely allied to egotism; and excessive sensibility is only another name for morbid self-consciousness. The cure for tender sensibilities is to make more of our objects and less of our selves.

CHRISTIAN NEVELL BOVEE
AUTHOR AND LAWYER

Self-consciousness is the mortal enemy of focus and concentration. If you are thinking about how you may be perceived, you can't give your complete focus to the situation at hand. Self-consciousness has to do with the future rather than the present.

What's the worst that could happen? Identify in your *Per-*

sonal Brilliance Notebook the worst possible scenarios to your situation. Examples may be, "I'll look stupid" or "They won't respect me." Now, create a list of all of the potential positive outcomes. If you have ten negatives make sure you have ten positives. Then, let it go. Focus on the process, not on yourself. Stay in the present.

Life Balance

Wisdom is your perspective on life, your sense of balance, your understanding of how the various parts and principles apply and relate to each other. It embraces judgment, discernment, and comprehension. It is a gestalt or oneness, and integrated wholeness.

STEPHEN R. COVEY
SPEAKER, TRAINER, AND AUTHOR

The pursuit of living a balanced life has become a trendy idea and one of the latest crazes. The irony is that many people are becoming more stressed out than ever before as they attempt to balance the various areas of life. While I agree that "all work and no play makes Jack a dull boy," I don't believe that life can be neatly compartmentalized.

The reality is that one area of life seamlessly flows to and from the others, and when you grasp what this concept offers, you won't want it to be any other way! For example, I recently spoke at a leadership seminar and decided to stay for the afternoon session. The topic was life balance and the speaker was a psychologist. Her first exercise for the group was to have us break our time down for a week, on a percentage basis, among categories like time spent on work, family, health, hobbies, and ourselves. The idea was that if we could have fairly equal percentages we were healthy. If we were lacking in a particular area it showed where we needed some work. Sounded good.

I tried the exercise but quickly became very frustrated. I just couldn't break my time down that way.

One example is golf, which is a hobby and a passion. I work out with specific exercises to support my hobby. I often walk and carry my bag. A round is about six miles of walking. Is this health? I've built hugely successful personal and business relationships with people I've met while playing golf. Is this business or friendship? My family also plays, so we play together. Is this family time? Is this a hobby? Is this work? Is this personal time? I couldn't figure out how to do the exercise.

I was so frustrated, I stood up and asked the question, "Doctor, I'm really having trouble with this exercise, can I get some help?" She responded, "Perhaps you should set up an appointment with my office." Kidding aside, as we discussed the issue as a group, she adapted her presentation to acknowledge that there is more than one kind of balance.

Just as the catalysts of awareness, curiosity, focus, and initiative work together seamlessly, not sequentially, I believe that we should seek a seamless balance to our lives.

Beware of compartmentalization disguised as balance. By an extreme definition of life balance (which is easy to grasp and which many "experts" are pushing), you aren't even allowed to have an idea while taking a shower. That's a problem—since a recent study indicated that the shower was the number one place for great ideas.

A Narrow Focus

Some people see more in a walk around the block than others see in a trip around the world.

ANONYMOUS

Expand your focus. Take a walk in the park or around your neighborhood. Start in a laser-focused way by paying close attention to your steps. One step after another. Notice your gait. Notice how each foot hits the ground. After a few minutes, expand your focus to notice your breath. What is the pace of your breathing? Now, notice how many colors you can see around you on your walk. Do you still have a sense of your steps? Next, expand your attention to focus on both your steps and your breath. Yes, you can do both at once. On your walk continue to notice additional things using all of your senses. Regularly go back to the steps and breathe. Practice moving your focus around.

Interruptions

*Circumstances may cause interruptions and delays,
but never lose sight of your goal. Prepare yourself in every
way you can by increasing your knowledge and adding to
your experience, so that you can make the most of
opportunity when it occurs.*

MARIO ANDRETTI
AUTO RACER

To a certain extent dealing with interruptions is a matter of choice. If you choose not to allow the interruptions to sidetrack you, they won't. If you are on purpose and decide to overcome interruptions, you can do it. For the next week, identify the types of interruptions you encounter through the day. Where do they come from? Are there any consistencies? What was your reaction to the interruption? Use your *Personal Brilliance Notebook* to record your observations. Develop a creative action plan to put an approach in place to more productively take advantage of your interruptions.

An observational study on the nature of interruptions in

the workplace shows that in most cases (64 percent) the person being interrupted received some benefit from the interruption. This supports our definition of focus. By being open to input from all areas, even interruptions, our experience is much richer, bringing these various inputs to bear on our situation.

However, the finding from the study that is most significant to us is that in just over 40 percent of interruptions, the person being interrupted did not resume the work they were doing prior to the interruption. Assuming what you were working on was important, not getting back to it is a serious problem. You need to be able to quickly turn back your focus to the subject at hand.

We discussed the creation of a trigger mechanism in Chapter 12 to get back into focus quickly and easily. Continue to practice your trigger mechanism.

Just as with athletic training, it is valuable to simulate game conditions while performing skill enhancement drills. The following eavesdropping exercise is designed to put you in a position of having many interruptions while trying to maintain focus, with a few added complications. The exercise is intended to help develop your focus muscles. Only try it if you are comfortable with it and can have some fun. It's not intended to invade privacy or cause problems in any way. Use your best judgment.

Focus Exercise

In a crowded restaurant with tables in close proximity, chose a table that is close to a table of four or more diners. A group of four or more people probably won't be discussing any intimate subjects. While maintaining complete stealth, listen in to their conversation and try to pick up the thread of the subject matter. You don't know the parties, so you may have to use your imagination to fill in the blanks. While trying to make sense of their conversation, read the menu, order your meal, look around naturally, and continue your interaction with your meal partner. The natural interruptions in a restaurant will test your ability to focus. You also must intensify your hearing to listen over the background noise. This exercise also tests your ability to focus on the periphery of your senses. Have a little fun with this, but again, be careful. If the conversation seems to be getting into a confidential area, suspend the exercise and try again later.

Physiology

I never stay away from workouts. I work hard. I've tried to take care of my body. I'll never look back and say that I could have done more. I've paid the price in practice, but I know I get the most out of my ability.

CARL YASTRZEMSKI
BASEBALL PLAYER

Take good care of yourself. Eat right and get plenty of exercise—yes, these are clichés but that doesn't mean the advice is any less valid. On top of all the other benefits, you'll find that your ability to focus improves dramatically.

Don't skip a meal when on deadline. My Italian mother made this rule very clear, even without the scientific studies. It's easy to get caught up in the excitement of a potentially brilliant idea and find that we missed a meal. Consistent nutrition is necessary to keep the engine going productively. Remember that you can't focus effectively for long periods of time. Meals are natural break points. Avoid fast food. Stop, sit down, and eat. The break will pay off in the long run.

Many people suffer from food allergies to processed foods. The symptoms could be subtle, like a slight dullness in focus. We tend to take it for granted as normal. See a nutritionist who can analyze your diet to see what effect it might have on your mental and physical energy.

*   *   *

In the next chapter, we'll look at a variety of exercises you can use to expand your focus.

CHAPTER 14

Expanding FOCUS

Bring ideas in and entertain them royally, for
one of them may be the king.

MARK VAN DOREN
AUTHOR

EXPANDING your focus is one of the most powerful things you can do to enjoy greater success in all areas of life. By expanding your focus, you exponentially increase your possibilities, because a 360-degree vision takes in all of the available options and shows you how information can be used separately or in tandem for the most successful results.

AWARENESS
CURIOSITY
FOCUS
INITIATIVE

While breaking through focus barriers involves strengthening your weak links, expanding your focus is about refining and enlarging your current abilities. The power of expanding your focus will enable you to take quantum leaps toward your definition of success.

Arm & Hammer Baking Soda provides a real life exercise that helps expand focus. To increase the usage of their product that's been in existence for 155 years, the company identified the numerous uses for baking soda. Their Web site offers tips for how to use their product in various areas of the home, for your family, and for your body. At this writing there are more than 100 tips available for how baking soda can be used.

A great way to begin to expand your focus and also use the other personal brilliance catalysts is to think of uses for a product other than the intended use. This process causes you to focus, not only on the intricate components of the product, but also on the environment in which it's used.

Quick Exercise

Read the following sentence just once with your focus tuned in and count the number of times the letter *f* occurs in the sentence:

Freedom fighters are effective as a result of years of difficult study combined with the experience of years.

If you counted less than nine *f*s, perhaps your eyes took the learned short cut that many do and skipped the word "of." The scary part is the opportunity cost—we don't know what we miss.

This chapter is about practice. There are a number of exercises designed to simulate the various aspects of attention, concentration, and focus. The more experience you have, the better you will perform. If your physical body is well trained and fit, it can expend more energy or power over a shorter period of time. You can lift more weight, run faster, jump higher, require less rest, and be healthier. The same holds true for your mind's energy. Your ability to focus, which is the gathering filter for the brain, can be expanded through mental training and exercise. The mental power you develop will help improve concentration, heighten your imagination, and help solve problems. In effect, you will be able to focus better, generating all of the benefits increased focus brings.

Practice Interval Training

If you train hard, you'll not only be hard,
you'll be hard to beat.

HERSCHEL WALKER
ALL-AMERICAN FOOTBALL PLAYER

Interval training is a way to step up the intensity of an aerobic workout. The idea behind it is to increase the intensity of the workout for a brief interval followed by a recovery period and then repeating the intense workout interval. You can use interval training in your focus workout as well.

Choose a task associated with a problem or opportunity you are working on. For illustration purposes, let's say it involves reading an academic report and creating a summary for your colleagues at work. The report is dry and boring and is not something you want to read.

You can start out slow. Set an alarm to time the intervals. Create a clean environment, laying out the report and your *Personal Brilliance Notebook*. For this task you'll want a dictionary close by as well. Try to remove as much clutter around you as you can. Sit quietly and move into a relaxed state. Clear your mind as much as possible. You don't need to think about the task. Just let your mind relax.

Now, set the timer for two minutes. Execute the trigger mechanism you created in Chapter 12. Begin reading the report and jot down any notes or ideas in your *Personal Brilliance Notebook* as they occur to you. Focus on your reading as best as you can. If other thoughts enter your mind, dismiss them and get your focus back. If you encounter a word that you are not familiar with, look it up in the dictionary. When time is up, stop reading. Set the timer again for two minutes and move back into your relaxed state and clear mind. This time, if thoughts about the report enter into your mind, just accept them.

Repeat the two-minute intervals of focus and relaxation twice. Then, increase the intervals to four minutes. Over time, you should be able to increase the focus time to fifteen, then twenty, then thirty minutes. With interval training, the break time is just as important as the focus time. Remember, you're training for real life when you'll have to turn your focus on and off as interruptions occur.

Learn to Meditate

Through meditation and by giving full attention to one thing at a time, we can learn to direct attention where we choose.

EKNATH EASWARAN
AUTHOR AND PROFESSOR

In many ways, meditation is the opposite of focus, in that you are letting go, relaxing your mind, and turning down the volume of the many messages flying through. On the other hand, meditation is a practice of concentration and focus. There are many forms of meditation available. For those of you who are unsure about jumping into meditation because of its mystical side, or because it sounds difficult, many writers and coaches have made the practice much easier to get into than ever before. Find the approach that feels comfortable to you.

Personally, I meditate with the aid of an audiotape that provides a sound equivalent to the theta and delta rhythms of our brains. This allows me to easily enter into a meditative state, with very little training or effort. There is a great deal of our mental muscle that is unused. I believe meditation is a way to tap into that resource.

Use Visualization Techniques

To accomplish great things we must first dream, then
visualize, then plan . . . believe . . . act!

ALFRED A. MONTAPERT
AUTHOR

Visualization is a very powerful mental training technique. Basically, visualization is the process of creating images in your mind. It is seeing the future or the past. Rather than telling yourself to perform well in your next activity, you actually see yourself performing well in your mind. Visualization takes away most of the surprises in any scenario. You've already seen it. Now you simply perform without the anxiety of the unknown. This allows you to focus on the experience.

My playing field is many times in a boardroom or an auditorium. By visualizing all of the possible nuances of a meeting or speech, as well as visualizing how I will react to different situations, I will be better prepared. In fact, I feel just as practiced as if I had actually done a dress rehearsal. With experience, the visualization is just as real in your mind as actually experiencing the event.

I did some testing of this concept myself. A few years ago I took a series of weekly golf lessons. At the end of each lesson the golf pro gave me drills to do between lessons. We started each lesson with a review. In effect, he graded me on how well I had mastered the material from the previous week. I found that if I practiced the drills at least three times between lessons, I could pass. I was traveling a great deal during this period. It was obvious that when I didn't do the drills he could instantly tell.

My experiment, without the golf pro's knowledge, was to use visualization. I did the drills in my mind, feeling the proper positions of my body, without a club, while sitting in a recliner. If I used visualization three times during the week instead of actual practice, I could at least pass the test. The golf pro could not tell the difference between when I physically did the drills and when I mentally did the drills. Of course, I had to swing the club at some point, but when I did I was practicing the correct movements because they were grooved in my mind.

There are two types of visualization. *Subject visualization* is when you are the subject of the visualization. You are visualizing yourself performing. My example above of the golf lesson visualization was subject visualization. This works best in a performance scenario because your body actually experiences the visualized movements.

A second type of visualization is *object visualization,* in which you view the action as if you are watching a movie. With practice, you can combine both types of visualization in one session. For example, when I'm visualizing a speech I am delivering, I perform and see what is happening from my eyes as the presenter, and then also see the whole environment (myself included) so I can anticipate reactions from different perspectives.

Visualization Tips

- Choose a quiet time and place with little chance of interruption for your visualization.
- Practice visualization using all of your senses and see the action in color if possible. The more vivid, the better. Use your senses to make it as real as you can.
- Use whatever props are necessary to help bring the visualization to life. For example, if I can visit the auditorium prior to the speech I can use the real image in my visualization. In the golf example, it was very helpful to see a video of myself performing the drills correctly.
- Correct any failures in your visualization. This is practice

time. Practice a flawless performance. However, also practice your response to possible difficult situations that may arise. Visualize your strong, confident, positive reaction.
- Visualize regularly. Repetition of a specific visualization is necessary. You will also get better at the process of visualization with practice.

Visualization doesn't replace hard work. Think of it as a secret weapon that enhances preparation and hard work.

Look and Listen with Intent

Success in life is founded upon attention to the small things rather than to the large things; to the every day things nearest to us rather than to the things that are remote and uncommon.

BOOKER T. WASHINGTON
AFRICAN-AMERICAN LEADER AND EDUCATOR

The human body and our senses are truly remarkable. It's easy though to take them for granted. Our finely tuned senses allow us to watch TV, talk on the phone, and notice the smell of dinner cooking in the next room. It's important to be conscious of our senses periodically to appreciate our own complexity while practicing focus.

I just came in from walking the dog. She is very well trained, so she walks off-leash. She actually sits and waits at each corner for the OK to cross the street. When I am walking ahead of her, I try to guess on what side she will approach me as she runs to catch up. I use the jingle of her collar (listening). I try to sense her approach as she enters my space (feel). Looking ahead, I note what she might find interesting that would cause her to go to one side or the other (pattern recognition). This game helps me with my focus. Can you devise a similar exercise to test these things? Perhaps you might guess where people are going to sit at your next staff meeting based on habit, power struggles, who is working together, etc.

You've no doubt heard that you should think positive thoughts! Before you jump to that advice, take the time to find out what's actually going on in your mind. What are you actually saying to yourself? You can't change it until you are aware of it. In a relaxed atmosphere, use your *Personal Brilliance Notebook* to record your self-talk. Yes, listen to yourself; focus on your inner dialogue. Try to observe your thoughts without censoring them. Review the day. Write down your experience. Also write down what you were feeling at the time and what you were saying to yourself at that point. Review your notes and determine if some of your internal language should be changed.

What about focusing on what someone else is saying to you? This is critical to expanding your focus. Here are some tips for active listening. Try them in conversations over the next week and notice the difference.

1. Surrender to the moment of the speaker. Absorb her presentation with all of your senses.
2. Consciously attempt to suspend the mental chatter that occurs as you are preparing to talk next.
3. Suspend judgment. Your opinions and reactions create static. Just listen.
4. Empathize with the speaker. Why is she saying this? What is most important to the speaker?
5. Identify the essence of the speaker's message, homing in on the most important point.

Focus Exercises

Exercise #1
Try to look into the eyes of a partner for two minutes without blinking. Set a timer. This is not a contest. The idea is to

listen with your eyes. What do you see? When the timer goes off, relax and reflect on the experience. Ask your partner to explain their experience. Compare notes. Use your *Personal Brilliance Notebook* to describe the experience.

Exercise #2

In the next TV show or movie you watch, focus on a background character for a change of pace. Can you pay attention to the extra and still understand the story line?

Watch a baseball or soccer game and focus on the umpires or referees. Note the different perspective you have on the game.

Exercise #3

Select a picture, painting, or computer-generated graphic. You can use the graphic associated with this book, available online at: *www.MyPersonalBrilliance.com/graphic.* Set aside a half-hour in which you will not be interrupted. Be sure to suspend your screen saver as you will be focusing on the image for at least thirty minutes. Make yourself comfortable in front of your computer screen. Look at the graphic for at least ten minutes without moving even one small muscle or giving in to even one tiny adjustment. Keep your eyes and your mind on the image. If your mind begins to wander off in a chain of associations, keep coming back to the picture. You can expect that many things can be found in the image that you have previously not noticed.

After ten or fifteen minutes, turn away from the graphic and recall what you have experienced, step by step. Make this as visual as possible; review the experience visually rather than with words. After the exercise, go about the day's work, trying to recall the experience when you can.

Learn a Foreign Language

To have another language is to possess a second soul.

CHARLEMAGNE
KING OF THE FRANKS; EMPEROR OF THE WEST

Learning a foreign language requires focused listening. Understanding the spoken word in the new language is our highest priority, so listening naturally becomes more focused. Jot down in your *Personal Brilliance Notebook* what this level of concentration feels like. Can you apply this feeling to conversations in your primary language? Learning a foreign language exercises four different areas of learning: listening, speaking, reading, and writing. The added bonus is that you will be armed with the new language when visiting the new country. You can really stretch your innovation muscles then.

Following are some tips for sharpening your focus.

Sharpen Your Focus

- Fine-tune your intensity. Focus gently and guard against obsession.
- Allow time for ideas to simmer while you do other things.
- Direct your focus appropriately. Find a balance between physical and cerebral pursuits, easy and challenging activities, and solitude and activities with others.
- Let go of things that sap your energy. Prioritizing helps you to be sure you're focusing on the right things.
- Really listen to others with focus. So often, we go through the motions and miss opportunities to learn. What are the person's eyes telling you? What about her body language? Is it consistent with the words you're hearing?
- Live, work, and play with intention.

INITIATIVE

CHAPTER 15

The Power of INITIATIVE

*Let him who would move the world, first
move himself.*

SOCRATES
GREEK PHILOSOPHER

WITHOUT HARNESSING the power of initiative, the wheel of innovation comes to a screeching halt. While awareness, curiosity, and focus are essential elements to personal brilliance, without the motivation to move forward, very little happens. We all have a desire to "make a difference" or to make improvements in our lives, but for a variety of reasons, when it comes to taking initiative many people face a variety of challenges.

> AWARENESS
> CURIOSITY
> FOCUS
> **INITIATIVE**

Fortunately, there are many things you can do to enhance your power of initiative, and the payoffs are huge. How many times have you, or someone you know, come up with a great idea, but didn't act on it, only to discover down the road that someone else seized the opportunity and ran with it? For example, one of my friends, who is a counselor and a published author, had an idea several years ago to write a book about "excavating" the powerful core of who we really are. She knew there was a market for the idea because most people are looking for something more out of life. She toyed with the idea, but didn't take it any further. A year later

Sarah Ban Breathnach released her blockbuster hit, *Something More: Excavating Your Authentic Self.*

The power of initiative is a critical catalyst for personal brilliance. You need it to bring your dreams to life, but it's also necessary in order to start the innovation process. Without the motivation to amplify your awareness, explore your curiosities, or expand your focus, you probably won't even make it to the drawing board, let alone come up with a new idea or solution.

Taking Initiative

There are four primary behaviors needed to successfully take initiative:

1. Identifying meaningful internal and external motivators
2. Aligning goals with personal and professional values
3. Reducing or allaying fears associated with your goals
4. Taking the first action step, followed by as many steps as it takes to reach the goal

Meaningful Motivators Feed Initiative

> *If necessity is the mother of invention, discontent is the father of progress.*
>
> DAVID ROCKEFELLER
> BUSINESS LEADER

Let's face it, if you don't have a good reason to accomplish a particular goal, you probably won't do it. A good reason is what I call a "meaningful motivator," and these compelling reasons are the fuel that initiative needs to grow and thrive.

They keep our minds from stopping us short with internal arguments that play the part of nay-sayers. For example, if you have an idea to write a book, but you can't connect that idea to a meaningful outcome, you're likely to put off that goal.

There are two primary types of motivation: internal and external. Depending on the goal you have in mind, one or the other may work to get you going. Using the example of book writing, if you have a burning desire to simply write a book whether anyone else ever reads or buys it, that *internal* motivation might be enough to propel you forward. If your motivation is primarily *external*, such as getting the book published or self-publishing it and selling a ton of copies, you'll probably need to know that your desired outcome is feasible before you'll take the goal seriously and actually sit down to do the work.

Research studies, together with my business and personal experiences, have convinced me that a balance of internal and external motivators is the most powerful combination to feed your initiative and get the ball rolling. In my case, I had a deep desire to share the information and insights that I speak about almost daily in the form of a book that would make a difference in more people's lives. That was my internal motivator. I also found a writing coach with connections in the publishing industry who firmly believed that my book was worthy of publication. When I found a literary agent who shared my coach's belief in my project, my initiative went from moderate to high practically overnight. With the internal and external motivators in place, I was excited to move from idea into action, and the result is the book you're holding in your hands right now.

On its own, neither the internal nor the external motivator would have been enough for me to carve time out of my schedule to do the writing. I know this because I'd been approached by literary agents and publishers in the past to write books that I simply wasn't inspired to write. Although they were practically guaranteeing me that the books they had in mind would sell, I just wasn't excited about their ideas. The internal motivation, in terms of this book, also wasn't enough to really get me going. Although I was inspired to share what I've learned, if no one ever bought or read the book, the process felt pointless to me. It was only when *both* the internal and external motivators were in place that I got serious about reaching this goal.

The key to moving from idea to action is to identify what it will take to make the goal worth achieving. Once you are aware of your internal and external motivators, your mind begins to connect the process with the success of achieving your goal.

Goals Plus Values Equal Action Steps

You have got to know what it is you want! Or someone is going to sell you a bill of goods somewhere along the line that will do irreparable damage to your self-esteem, your sense of worth, and your stewardship of talents that God gave you.

RICHARD NELSON BOLLES
WHAT COLOR IS YOUR PARACHUTE?

Pursuing a goal that's in conflict with your value system is kind of like trying to squeeze your feet into shoes that are a size too small. You may be able to hobble around in them for a while, but it will only be a matter of time before the discomfort is so great, you'll have no other logical choice but to remove the shoes.

I came across a great example of this while coaching a woman whose goal was to be one of the top salespeople in her health insurance agency and to win the annual trip to Hawaii. She said she went into insurance sales because in her previous job—as an administrative assistant in a local hospital—she learned that many people couldn't afford the recommended medical treatment because they didn't have insurance that adequately covered their costs. She said, "When I sell insurance, I educate people to get the policies that will allow them to get the right medical treatment without having to go into debt." Her internal motivation was strong and at first glance it appeared that she had a goal that was in line with her values.

However, when I asked her what sort of health insurance policy she had for herself, she admitted that her policy would not cover her needs for many of the tests, medications, and treatments that were associated with common health problems. Her rationalization was, "I'm almost never sick and I don't want to spend hundreds of dollars each month on a policy that I'm not using." Probing deeper, I learned that she followed a rather strict regimen of holistic health. She took about twenty vitamins and supplements each day, grew and juiced her own wheat grass, practiced yoga and meditation, and really had some issues with modern medicine.

I decided that to get to the bottom of this, it would be necessary for me to go on a few sales calls with her. What I witnessed would make great material for a sitcom. Instead of trying to sell her prospects a policy that would fully cover them, she spent a good deal of her appointment time educating them about ways to stay healthy. She actually talked two couples out of buying a policy altogether, referring them to her naturopathic doctor instead. Her goal to be the top saleswoman in her insurance office was clearly out of sync with her values. After all, having a firm belief in a product is the foundation of selling that product with conviction and enthusiasm.

Rather than help this woman reach her goal, I helped her

to create a new goal that would be supported by her values. Within three months she had a new job as a community relations director at the holistic clinic to which she had referred so many of her previous insurance prospects. She thrived in this role and was excited to share her knowledge in community forums, health awareness programs, and by working one on one to educate patients about their treatment options. She also introduced a new health product to the clinic and earned a commission on the sales. Within two years she had earned enough in commissions alone to take her entire family to Hawaii.

The bottom line here is to get real with yourself. Before you can set and work toward achieving your goals, it's essential to be very clear about your own values and beliefs. (In Chapters 17 and 18, you'll have an opportunity to complete a few exercises that will assist you in identifying and clarifying your values.)

Getting Clear About Your Fears

You may be disappointed if you fail, but you are doomed if you don't try.

BEVERLY SILLS
SOPRANO AND OPERA DIRECTOR

A great old saying is that worrying is like sitting in a rocking chair. It gives you something to do but it doesn't get you anywhere. If you were to add up all of the time and energy you've invested over your lifetime worrying about things that never came to pass, you'd be astonished to see how wasteful this habit can be.

When we're worried about a potentially negative outcome or situation, we spin our mental wheels going around and around in circles, kind of like a hamster on one of those cage toys that look like miniature Ferris wheels. Hamsters need those wheels to use up some of the energy that can't possibly be expended by walking around their cages. Humans, on the other hand, particularly in today's fast-paced world, need to conserve energy and use it wisely in ventures that yield real results.

Quick Experiment

It's been estimated that the majority of people spend more than 70 percent (some research indicates the percentage is actually closer to 85 percent) of their waking time thinking about the past and the future. If this sounds extreme to you, do a little experiment. Set a timer to go off every thirty minutes for an entire day. Each time the alarm goes off, write down the thought you were having at that precise moment the alarm sounded. And don't cheat. What you'll probably find at the end of the day is that the majority of the thoughts you recorded were focused in past or future. As we discussed in the chapters on awareness, present-time thinking is essential for identifying goals, solving problems, and formulating effective action plans.

Time and energy that's wasted by focusing on fears, worries, and potentially negative outcomes can be wisely spent by training yourself to return to the present moment over and over again, regardless of the situation or problem that you are facing. No one is a natural-born worrier. Worrying and being fearful are behaviors that we learn. Therefore, these behaviors can be "un-learned." Just like any other habit, learning not to worry and not to dwell on fear is a process that needs to be practiced for it to become a new habit. (In Chapter 17, you'll have a chance to start honing this skill.)

The main reason that worry, fear, and other negative emotions impede initiative is that you can't effectively move forward when you're afraid to find out what's beyond the next door or around the next corner.

A client named John, who recently joined one of our coaching programs, has been talking about setting up a digital photography business for going on five years. His major in college was photography and since then he has had a great deal of experience in the field. When I met with him, I learned—through much prying and cajoling—that the reason he hadn't moved forward with his plan was that he didn't understand how to use a computer and was afraid that he wouldn't be able to learn. Now, this is a really smart guy, who's learned plenty of stuff that many people can't begin to comprehend. But his fear of feeling stupid and being embarrassed was stopping him from enrolling in a computer course. He's more of an introvert than an extrovert, and the idea of sitting in a classroom felt extremely uncomfortable and distasteful to him.

I sat with John and helped him to estimate how much money he might earn in one year with a digital photography business. We then estimated how much money he would need to spend to hire a private computer coach to teach him what he needed to learn to get his business off the ground. Guess what? His investment for the learning curve was a pittance of his potential income; less than 5 percent! He looked at me in complete amazement and said, "I've been so stressed out about going to computer classes that it didn't even occur to me to hire a private coach!" Funny (actually not so funny!) what fear and worry can do to an otherwise intelligent and creative mind. An innovative solution is not that far away when you employ awareness, curiosity, focus, and initiative.

Taking the First Step

*All great masters are chiefly distinguished by the
power of adding a second, a third, and perhaps a fourth
step in a continuous line. Many a man had taken
the first step. With every additional step you
enhance immensely the value of your first.*

RALPH WALDO EMERSON
POET AND ESSAYIST

Taking action on ideas and goals that are important to us increases our self-confidence, improves our self-esteem, and has a profound impact on the level of personal power that we have at our disposal. In essence, the more we are actually doing the things we want to do, the better we feel about ourselves, and the better others feel about us.

One of the secrets to increasing initiative in your daily life is to shorten the time line between your idea and your first action step. As adults, many people have the tendency to put off that first step in favor of conducting more research, increasing their education, and basically trying to learn everything they need to know before they begin. If toddlers viewed the idea of standing up and walking the way many adults approach taking a first step, most people would still be crawling. Learning to increase your comfort with taking the first step toward any goal or objective will give you an edge over many of your potential competitors. People who reconnect with their innate sense of taking initiative are the ones who tend to accomplish the most and therefore experience the greatest deal of self-satisfaction.

I saw this concept in action several years ago when I agreed to participate in a demonstration of something called a "High Ropes Course." A High Ropes Course is a series of obstacles placed forty feet up among the trees. There are balance beams to cross, nets to climb, rope bridges to traverse, and hanging rings to swing along. Before the course begins everyone is carefully instructed in safety precautions and outfitted with a harness that prevents them from falling. Even with all of these safety procedures and equipment, many people—because of their fear of heights—cannot successfully complete the course. In the ropes course that I took part in, the first obstacle was to cross a tree trunk that was about the width and length of a telephone pole. The tree trunk had flat pieces of wood nailed into the top of it so that we could step from one wooden foot platform to the next. The idea was to climb up the ladder to the platform in the tree and walk across the trunk to another platform at the opposite end.

I stood at the base of the ladder as the woman ahead of me—Marilyn—climbed up to the platform. There was no way that she could fall and get hurt because her harness was safely secured by a very strong rope to a guiding line. (The ropes are strong enough to suspend a compact car.) If she lost her balance, she would only fall a foot or two before the safety ropes caught her. Even so, she stood on top of the platform afraid to take the first step onto the tree trunk.

Our instructor, Gene, was encouraging her to take the first step, but Marilyn seemed frozen with fear. Gene said, "The longer you stand there thinking about taking that first step the harder it will become. Just allow yourself to take the first step and each step will be easier until you reach the other side." It sounded like great advice to me, but Marilyn said she needed to gather her courage. After standing up there for a few minutes, she actually began to shake—not the optimum thing to be doing when you're facing an obstacle that requires steadiness and balance. Eventually, she began to cry and decided to descend the ladder, turn in her gear, and hang out in the picnic area until the rest of us were finished.

When I reached the platform, I understood Marilyn's fear. It was definitely daunting to be forty feet above the ground, and looking down made it worse, especially since I don't usually even climb a ladder to change a light bulb. Gene stood at the bottom of the ladder and called up, "Jim, don't think about it. The longer you stand there, the harder it will be. Just step out onto the first foothold." He was the expert and I knew I was safe, and I guess because I just saw what failure looked like, I did as he said without waiting another second for more fear to build up. Within thirty seconds I had reached the opposite platform, feeling both relieved and confident that I could complete the other obstacles that were part of the course. That lesson made a big impact on how I now approach taking the first step in any goal that I have and in how I coach my clients. However, I still prefer to do this work while firmly planted on the ground.

*   *   *

Initiative is an integral catalyst to any form of innovation. In the chapters of this section we'll examine the natural capacity you have for taking initiative, share success stories of initiative paying off, identify some barriers to being a self-starter and ways to overcome them, and learn a few methods that can assist in harnessing the power of initiative.

CHAPTER 16

Get Ready, Get Set, GO!

Knowing is not enough; we must apply.
Willing is not enough; we must do.
JOHANN WOLFGANG VON GOETHE
GERMAN POET, DRAMATIST, AND NOVELIST

YOU have a creative idea, you're facing a challenge, or you're trying to solve a problem. What is it that motivates you to take the action steps to support your situation?

In the previous chapter we looked at the importance of having meaningful motivators, and we learned that in most cases a balance of internal and external motivation creates the spark you need to move an idea into action. However, there are situations in which just one type of motivation—whether internal or external—or a single event, is enough to get us going. An example of this might be a man who has never been able to stop smoking cigarettes, but quits immediately when his wife is diagnosed with lung cancer. Although his own health was not enough to make him stop, the external motivation of quitting for the sake of his wife's health does the trick.

Researchers in the area of human development and motivation have determined that for many people the incentive to stop pain is a stronger motivation than the incentive to increase pleasure. Les Brown, professional speaker and author,

AWARENESS
CURIOSITY
FOCUS
INITIATIVE

relays the following story to show how this type of motivation works.

> A young boy in a rural community is hired to deliver newspapers. Every day for a week when he delivers the paper to a farmhouse nearby, a big hound dog sits howling on the front porch. It's a terrible sound and the little boy who is a great dog lover is upset each time he stops at the farmhouse and hears the dog's painful howls. One day the farmer is out on the porch when the boy brings the paper. The young lad asks the farmer, "Why is your hound dog wailing like that?"
>
> The farmer answers, "Oh, old Duke there will be okay. He just sat on a nail."
>
> The boy is perplexed and asks, "Well, why doesn't he just get up off that nail?"
>
> The farmer's answer was startling in its simple logic: "Well, I guess it just doesn't hurt bad enough yet."

Interestingly, just as the elimination or reduction of pain can be a stronger motivating force than the pursuit of pleasure, what's missing in our lives often determines what we value the most at any given time. In a sense, our biggest voids become our greatest values. If you are single and lonely, your greatest void might be a partner, making the search for a mate your most important value. This same idea can be true in terms of increasing your income. Let's say that you have a desire to significantly increase your income. You know that by doing so, you will be able to afford to make home improvements, take the vacation of your dreams, or buy the sports car you've had your eye on. Even so, months and years go by and you don't take the steps to actually reach your goal.

Then one day you find out that one of your children is going to need a very expensive operation and that your insurance will only cover a fraction of the cost. Suddenly you are propelled into action. The idea of not being able to afford life-saving treatment for your loved one is just too painful to bear. Within weeks, you find a higher paying job and open a part-time business that will generate the amount of money that you need.

Of course, there are strong motivators that are not life-or-death situations, and the key is to determine what those motivators are for you. Everyone is different and what works for someone else may not do it for you. That's why identifying your own deepest voids and values is so important to increasing your level of initiative. It's important to note that your voids and values change throughout life. What was most important to you five years ago, or even a month ago, may not rank so highly today. Unless you are clear about what is truly most valuable to you, there is little chance that you will pursue achieving or obtaining it any time soon.

Taking Action Requires Support *and* Challenge

> If I had a formula for bypassing trouble, I wouldn't
> pass it around. Wouldn't be doing anybody a favor.
> Trouble creates a capacity to handle it. I don't say
> embrace trouble. That's as bad as treating it as an enemy.
> But I do say meet it as a friend, for you'll see a lot of it and
> had better be on speaking terms with it.
>
> OLIVER WENDELL HOLMES, SR.
> PHYSICIAN, AUTHOR, AND POET

When it comes to taking initiative, support and challenge are equally important. If I were *talking* to you right now, rather than writing, I would repeat that statement two or three times until it had a chance to really sink in. That's how critical this idea is to the topic of becoming more of a self-starter.

Many of the people I meet tell me that if only they had more support and less challenge, they could get their idea off the ground. Wrong! Not surprisingly, I've never met anyone who says they wish they had more challenge and less support. It seems that many people, if not most, embrace a fairy-tale version of what it actually takes to initiate a new idea, concept, or business.

For the sake of argument, let's say that you have every single resource you believe you need to start a new business: money, supplies, office space, furniture, equipment, and even clients. In addition, you are surrounded by a group of people who totally believe in what you plan to do, and not one of them is disputing your ideas or questioning your business plan. Under this fantasy scenario, what will motivate you into action? If you already have everything you need, where's the incentive to begin a business that will bring you more? By all means create a support network to assist you in reaching your goals. But, only support without challenge can result in complacency.

The reality of people who are self-starters is that they use their lack of resources to propel them into action. They embrace the challenge. They have a burning internal drive to succeed, and they use that drive to garner support for their new venture, including finding investors and coming up with the necessary material resources. Some of the most impressive success stories often begin with little or no money or resources. The desire to have those things is what makes these entrepreneurs work harder and smarter. People who have achieved success over and over again go out of their way to find staff members and advisors who will challenge their ideas and tear their business plans to pieces. They want to hear every objection and be aware of as many potential pitfalls as humanly possible. They don't let the challenges get them down; they use them to skip a few steps on the way up!

A fabulous example that illustrates this concept is a twenty-nine-year-old entrepreneur whom I recently had the pleasure of meeting. Wil Schroter contacted me to pick my brain about my professional speaking business. Although he is already succeeding in his own speaking career, he wanted me to question and challenge the approach he's taking and shoot as many holes in his plan as I could. He was looking for me to challenge what could be better and affirm what he was doing well. Support and challenge. Did I mention that this guy is a self-made multimillionaire? If you still think you need more support than challenge to launch a successful venture, you're about to be humbled in your thinking.

At age 19, while still a student at the Ohio State University, Wil founded his first company from the confines of his dorm room. Within months of starting Blue Diesel, an interactive marketing agency, Wil's clients included Best Buy, BMW, and Eli Lilly. In less than six years, Wil grew this company to more than $65 million in capitalized billings. At the end of 2002, he sold Blue Diesel to an advertising agency holding company. In 1997, while still growing Blue Diesel, Wil had co-founded a technology consulting company called Kelltech Internet Services. Three years later he sold Kelltech for a cool $10 million. Wil is proud to be a very successful serial entrepreneur who has welcomed challenge all along the way. His success story just goes on and on, and today one of his roles is as CEO of Swapalease.com, aggressively leading the company's market-dominant position as the world's largest online automobile leasing marketplace.

There is absolutely no question that a balance of support and challenge propels you forward with the greatest force.

To Compete or Not to Compete?

There is nothing noble in being superior to someone else.
The true nobility is in being superior to your previous self.

HINDU SAYING

Although many people have nothing good to say about competition, just as many others sing its praises. So what's the answer? Quite simply, it depends on who you are. There is no right or wrong answer. Competition increases initiative for some and stifles it for others.

If your tendency is to be more independent than cooperative, more dominant than accepting, and more driven than relaxed, chances are that competition will fire you up and incite your personal sense of initiative. If, on the other hand, you tend to be more accepting than dominant, more relaxed than driven, and prefer cooperation or teamwork over working independently, then competition will most likely stress you out and possibly even frighten you. This is yet another area where awareness plays a starring role. You have to know your own preferences and tendencies to make a wise choice as to whether competition will be good for your sense of initiative or have the opposite effect.

People who have high levels of dominance and personal drive thrive on competition, because winning is one of the ways they increase their sense of self-worth. If people like this lose a competition, they don't throw in the towel. They sign up for the next round and try even harder to win. Although they really love to win, losing doesn't discourage or deflate them, it motivates them to improve. The participants of the popular television series *Survivor* are clearly in this group. They practically salivate at the thought of pitting themselves against others and facing what most people would consider outrageous odds.

On the other hand, people who have very accepting per-
sonalities and are typically more relaxed than driven shrink
in the face of most competition. They don't link their self-
worth to winning, but rather to cooperating and being a team
player. Their motto is, "All for one and one for all." If someone with this type of personality loses a competition, it can
have a negative impact for days, weeks, or longer. I shudder
to think of the emotional turmoil that some of the "losers" on
the *American Idol* show must experience after being raked
over the coals on national television by Simon.

It's important to point out that many people feel comfortable and motivated by competing in some arenas, and abhor
the idea of competing in others. The key is to be honest with
yourself and determine whether a particular form of competing is going to work in your favor or against you.

You Don't Have to Be Inspired to Begin

Do the thing, and you will have the power.

RALPH WALDO EMERSON
POET AND ESSAYIST

Contrary to some new-age philosophies, you don't need to be
inspired about a project or idea to get it going. Of course,
being inspired can help an awful lot, but inspiration and initiative are a little like the controversy over whether the
chicken or the egg comes first. The truth is that starting a new
project or pursuing a goal can spark inspiration even if you
were initially devoid of enthusiasm. For example, the thought
of starting a new exercise routine may trigger a desire to pull
the covers over your head and stay in bed all day. So, do you
wait until you feel inspired to head for the gym or the health
spa, or do you commit to going in spite of your lack of excite-

ment? When it comes to developing initiative, the latter is clearly the correct response.

Many times, inspiration doesn't come until after we have immersed ourselves in a project or made a firm commitment to a goal. Sometimes we don't feel the least bit inspired until we begin to see results or can see the light at the end of the proverbial tunnel. Many people in weight-loss programs can attest to this. They sign up for a weight-loss program and begin the new regimen, hating every bit of it. But as the weight begins to come off, and they like the look and energy of their slimming physique, the inspiration to keep going begins to grow. In many ways, initiative itself leads to inspiration. As the author Peter de Vries wisely stated, "I write when I'm inspired, and I see to it that I'm inspired at nine o'clock every morning." Anyone who writes for a living can appreciate de Vries's sentiment.

There are as many roads to inspiration as there are to Rome. Or as a Zen master might say, there are 10,000 paths to the way. Let's get practical. Taking action steps is necessary to move forward on every one of those paths.

Necessity often creates another path to inspiration. There are scores of success stories that literally begin at the lowest point of a person's life or career. Some of the most life-altering inspirations are born in desperation's darkest hour. I remember hearing a man named Paul as he addressed a group of United Way supporters. Paul had been a successful businessman at the top of his sales game. He shared that his life had seemed perfect. He had everything he wanted; a great job, a loving wife, and plenty of money to meet his needs. And then alcohol entered the picture. He began as a social drinker and soon found that he was drinking every day. Although his boss, colleagues, friends, and wife pleaded with him to seek help, he felt invincible and continued his daily habit.

Eventually, he lost his job, his wife, and almost lost his

life. He said he was living in a homeless shelter, scraping up whatever change he could find to buy his daily bottle of cheap liquor. One night, at the end of his rope, he began to wish he were dead. When he saw his reflection in a mirror, he didn't even recognize himself. It wasn't until he had hit rock bottom and was in the pits of desperation that he saw the light. He said he fell to his knees and began to pray. After a few minutes, he heard a knock at his door. It was his ex-wife. She said she doesn't know what prompted her to go to him that night. It had been months since she'd seen him.

He recalled that seeing her shining face in his doorway was like seeing an angel. He enrolled in a recovery program and never took another drink. He also devoted his life to helping other alcoholics to heal and has been instrumental in helping thousands of people through sharing his story and encouraging others to reconnect with the people and things in life that are most meaningful to them. Was Paul inspired to stop drinking when he checked himself into a rehab facility? No. Is he inspired now? You bet.

Another source of inspiration and initiative is information. There is a direct connection between what you learn and what you do. Being struck by lightning while flying a kite would have been a nightmare for most people. But for Benjamin Franklin, it was a revelation. Newton was certainly not the first person to sit under a tree and have an apple fall on his head. It was his knowledge and information that turned the event into an inspiration that radically changed the way we understand the world today. When the engineers at Xerox developed the technology of the computer mouse, their company saw no use for it. On the other hand, Apple Computer possessed information about the marketplace and what potential customers wanted. Including the mouse in Apple computers translated into hundreds of millions of dollars for the company.

By adding the catalyst of initiative to awareness, curiosity, and focus, you will be well on your way to turning your goals into accomplishments and your dreams into reality. Every man-made object that exists in our world began as a thought. But it wasn't thoughts that brought these ideas to life. It was the initiative of taking action. In the next two chapters, you will be guided through a series of action steps to help you to break through the barriers that impede your initiative and increase your ability to make self-starting a daily habit.

CHAPTER 17

Breaking Through Initiative BARRIERS

All men should thrive to learn before they die what they are running from, and to, and why.

JAMES THURBER
HUMORIST AND ILLUSTRATOR

YOU already have what it takes to get yourself moving, but chances are there are some barriers that are inhibiting your progress. Fear, limiting beliefs, perfectionism, and procrastination are some of the blocks that can interfere with your natural ability and desire to create positive change. Thankfully, each barrier that you break through will fuel your inner fire for greater accomplishment and reprogram your thinking so that "doing" becomes a way of life.

> AWARENESS
> CURIOSITY
> FOCUS
> **INITIATIVE**

The first step to breaking through initiative barriers is identifying your strongest blocks. Once you know what's in your way, you can begin to rewrite your old programming and creating a firmer foundation from which to take action steps. To identify your initiative barriers, read the descriptions that follow the list below and then note the ones that apply to you in your *Personal Brilliance Notebook*. Once you've determined your most prominent blocks, you can begin applying the strategies provided to break through those barriers.

Common Initiative Barriers

___Fear of failure
___Fear of success
___Limiting labels and beliefs
___Perfectionism
___Pessimism or resignation
___Procrastination
___Feeling overwhelmed

Fear of Failure

I don't know the key to success, but the key to failure is trying to please everybody.

BILL COSBY
COMEDIAN AND ACTOR

Fear of failing is one of the biggest barriers to starting a project or taking the next logical step in progressing toward a goal or an objective. As long as we don't do anything, we can hold onto the dream that we can succeed in our vision. If we actually begin the project, there's a fear that we'll discover that we can't do it, or that it can't be done. If you have a goal or a dream that you have been thinking and fantasizing about for more than a few months without taking a significant step forward, there's a chance that you are being paralyzed by a fear of failure.

Among the examples of this fear are the people who have a dream to be published, but who never actually begin their book or never submit their work to a literary agent or publisher. So long as they don't really put themselves out there, they can maintain the fantasy that "someday" they will be best-selling authors. The same goes for the people who say they want to be actors, but never audition for a single role, or the people who want to run a marathon, but haven't trained to successfully complete a 5K race or even a one-mile race.

Fear of Success

We fear our highest possibility (as well as our lowest one).
We are generally afraid to become that which we can
glimpse in our most perfect moments.

ABRAHAM MASLOW
EXISTENTIAL PSYCHOLOGIST

This one may surprise you. Many people stop short of pursuing a goal or beginning a project because they are afraid of how success may change their lives. Perhaps they are comfortable with the status quo and don't want to rock the boat. Sometimes people fear success because they think that if they succeed their friends and associates will be jealous of them or no longer like or accept them. Other people worry that if they reach a high level of success, they may outshine their mates or create a problem in their intimate relationships. Still others shy away from the success track because they have a negative perception of people whom they consider to be successful—leading to the "I-don't-want-to-turn-out-like-that" syndrome.

Another fear that stops a potentially successful project before it even begins is the fear that succeeding will mean a significant increase in current responsibilities or a decrease in free time. Almost always, people who have a fear of success are using black-and-white thinking, and are being stymied by their false perception of what success means.

Limiting Labels and Beliefs

The greatest obstacle to discovering the shape of the
earth, the continents, and the ocean was not ignorance, but
the illusion of knowledge.

DANIEL J. BOORSTIN
THE DISCOVERERS

A limiting label or belief is a false concept that a person is convinced is true, and that therefore isn't questioned. We can place *limiting labels* on situations as well as on people. Examples of limiting labels are that men are more capable leaders than women, that women are better caregivers than men, or that certain racial groups are smarter, and that others can't be trusted. The problem with this type of labeling is that some people tend to so firmly believe it that they have no inclination to look deeper or investigate the other possibilities. Since they are so sure they are correct, their minds can't even entertain the thought that they are inaccurate.

Limiting beliefs work the same way. When everyone was sure the world was flat, the idea of sailing out onto the ocean was considered ridiculous and meant certain death. Before the Wright brothers proved that flying was possible, the idea of flying was confined to science fiction stories. The same goes for traveling to the moon. Most people have at least a few limiting beliefs or labels. To discover your own, look at the beliefs that you hold dear or are adamant about, but have never actually researched or investigated.

Perfectionism

> *The pursuit of perfection often impedes improvement.*
>
> GEORGE WILL
> COLUMNIST, *THE WASHINGTON POST*

The word "perfect" means complete in all respects, without defects or omissions, regardless of how small or insignificant those defects or omissions may be. Perfectionism is extreme or obsessive striving for absolute perfection. So long as we're human, perfectionism is the equivalent of impossibility. And yet, there are many people plagued by perfectionism. There is a huge difference between striving to do our absolute best and trying to make something perfect.

Of course, I'm an advocate of doing the best we possibly can in every situation, but if our first step in a project has to be perfect, we'll never get to the second step. Some of the most valuable discoveries have occurred because of "imperfections" or mistakes made in the process of developing a product or a new idea. Many times projects are not started because a perfect result can't be guaranteed. If you find yourself frequently reworking a report or a project after it already meets or exceeds the objectives or specifications, you probably have a tendency toward perfectionism.

Pessimism or Resignation

> *Pessimism never won any battle.*
>
> DWIGHT D. EISENHOWER
> U.S. GENERAL AND PRESIDENT

Pessimism is the tendency to expect misfortune or the worst outcome in any circumstance. Resignation is the passive acceptance of a situation or circumstance. No one is born a pessimist. People learn to become pessimistic because of their environment and experiences. But even the worst circumstances in life don't make all people pessimistic. Clearly, pessimism is a learned perspective. Babies are not born with a sense of resignation. If a baby is hungry or wets its diaper, it doesn't just lie there and patiently wait until someone has the time to feed or change it. More likely, it cries and screams until its need are met.

Pessimists are known for statements like, "It will never work," "Yes, but . . . ," and "It can't be done." They don't just fear failure, they expect it. People who are resigned can be identified by statements like, "Why bother?" "It won't matter anyway," and "Just accept that things are the way they are." There is a difference between "doubt"—as was discussed in the Curiosity chapters—and pessimism. The likelihood of someone who is resigned or pessimistic starting a new venture or initiating a new idea is minimal at best.

Procrastination

All humanity is divided into three classes: those who are immovable, those who are movable, and those who move!

BENJAMIN FRANKLIN
STATESMAN AND PHILOSOPHER

Procrastination is the habit of putting off until tomorrow what you need or want to do today. For example, is there an item (or many) on your "things to do" list that you have been repeatedly rescheduling for days, weeks, or even months? Do you find yourself thinking and worrying about things that "must get done" but can't get yourself to do them? Are there library books, DVDs, videotapes, or other items in your home or office that are long overdue? These are all examples of procrastination. If you can relate to one or more of these illustrations, it's a good idea to commit to breaking through the procrastination barrier because this is one of the most pervasive stumbling blocks to initiative.

Feeling Overwhelmed

If you find a path with no obstacles, it probably doesn't lead anywhere.

FRANK A. CLARK
AUTHOR

The word "overwhelm" means to pour down over and cover or bury beneath. The second definition is to make helpless, as with greater force or deep emotion; to overcome, crush, or overpower. There are very few times in people's lives when they are actually buried or helpless. Yet, it seems half the people I encounter these days claim to be overwhelmed.

The feeling of being overwhelmed occurs when we believe that we are in over our heads, or that we are powerless to make a difference in a situation or circumstance. It's rarely a reality. Rather, it's a symptom of not knowing how to handle what we are facing or what has occurred. Feeling overwhelmed is sure to thwart our initiative because the idea of starting a new project is unthinkable if we believe that we already have too much to do.

Strategies for Breaking Through Initiative Barriers

Fear of Failure

> *I have not failed. I have (successfully) discovered*
> *twelve hundred materials that won't work.*
>
> THOMAS EDISON
> INVENTOR

If you have a fear of failure, begin with the worst outcome you can imagine and work backward. Let's say you have a report to complete for your boss and you are afraid that the report will not meet with her approval. So, what's the worst thing that can happen if that's true? Will you be fired? Will you be embarrassed or ridiculed? Will you be passed over for a possible promotion or be turned down for the raise you are counting on? Whatever the answer is for you, write it down, clearly and succinctly, in your *Personal Brilliance Notebook* and title it, "the worst-case scenario."

Next, look at what you have written and consider how this feared outcome might actually benefit you in some way. If your fear is being fired, would there be advantages to finding a new job? How many personal projects could you take care of while you are looking for your next job? Have you been entertaining the idea of starting your own business and, if so, might this be a great time to take steps in that direction? Would getting fired provide you with the incentive to start doing something that you enjoy more? It sounds silly at first, but give it a try.

Finally, make a list of people you know, or have heard or read about, who have experienced whatever you are most afraid will happen. Sticking with the example of being fired, what success stories have you heard about other people who lost their jobs? How did these people turn a "bad" thing into a "great" thing? You might be surprised to find out that many people who are highly successful have been fired at least once and sometimes more than once. I'm not suggesting that you actually change jobs at this point. The idea is to bring the fear into perspective so that it no longer stops or paralyzes your thinking and action steps.

Fear of Success

Most problems precisely defined are already partially solved.

HARRY LORAYNE
MEMORY MAKES MONEY

First of all, write down your definition of success. What does being successful mean to you and what does it entail?

Specifically clarify your worries or fears associated with achieving your definition of success. Allow yourself to write down all of your success fears, even if they seem illogical or absurd. If you have a fear of greater responsibility, elaborate on what those responsibilities might be, and how they could negatively affect you. If you're afraid of becoming like some of the successful people that you dislike, list the traits that you dislike and write a sentence explaining why you don't like those traits. The idea with this exercise is to be as concrete as possible. Once you have all of your fears down on paper, you have something tangible that you can work on. Sometimes just writing fears down brings them into the light of day and begins to put them into a more balanced perspective.

For each fear that you have listed, consider three ways that the potential problem can be managed or eliminated. For example, if you fear greater responsibility, what can you do to ease the potential burden? Some viable options might be to hire extra staff members, outsource more of the work, or hire subcontractors. Another option might be to work with an efficiency consultant or business coach who can teach you how to accomplish more in less time.

Limiting Labels and Beliefs

> *Common sense is the collection of prejudices*
> *acquired by age 18.*
>
> ALBERT EINSTEIN
> PHYSICIST

The challenge with identifying limiting labels and beliefs is that we tend to consider them "facts," rather than beliefs or prejudices. Therefore, we often have little or no clue that there is almost always a valid perspective that is in conflict with our own. If we are self-righteous in our stance, we may consider people who express an opposing view as stupid, ignorant, or uneducated.

To gain some experience in the area of expanding your own perspectives, write down a statement that you are certain is true. Do not write a statement that cannot currently be scientifically disproved, such as "We need air to breathe." Rather, zone in on an idea that you hold to be true. Some examples of "firm" beliefs include: "Cats are smarter than dogs" or "Children make marriage more satisfying" or "Lawyers are shysters." You get the idea.

Now, devote three hours of research and exploration to disputing your belief. Go to the library and check the facts. Search the Internet. Talk to friends and associates. Your goal is to compile a convincing case for the opposite side of your opinion. The more often you complete this exercise, the more expansive your thinking and belief system will become.

Perfectionism

If you can't make a mistake, you can't make anything.

MARVA N. COLLINS
EDUCATOR

One of the first steps to breaking through perfectionism is to begin editing the word "perfect" out of your vocabulary. Each time you think or say the word "perfect," correct yourself and substitute words like "excellent," "outstanding," and "impressive." If you have a spouse, partner, or close friend who is willing to help you with this, ask them to point out your usage of the word in your conversations with them. You might even come up with a nonverbal cue that they can use in public, such as raising their eyebrows, or placing a finger on their chin. You'll probably be surprised how frequently you use this word.

The next step to overcoming your perfectionism is to set firm deadlines for when a task or project must be completed. Estimate a realistic amount of time to accomplish the task and set your alarm to go off at the end of the time period. Similar to a timed test or a game show, when the alarm goes off, you are only permitted to complete the sentence you are writing or the nail you are hammering, and then you are done! Not only will this decrease your perfectionist tendencies, but it will also help you to set more realistic goals for how much time particular tasks actually take to complete.

Finally, to keep yourself accountable, make an agreement with your supervisor or a colleague that you will turn in the work or complete the task by the designated time. If this isn't enough to keep you accountable, commit to making a contribution to a charity or the pizza-party fund for each hour that the work is late.

There's a lot of truth to the idea that work expands to fill the amount of time we have to do it. If you don't have a firm deadline, you can revise and rework something forever. The idea is to commit to doing the very best job you can do in the time frame you have allotted.

Pessimism or Resignation

There are no hopeless situations; there are only people who have grown hopeless about them.

CLARE BOOTH LUCE
DIPLOMAT, DRAMATIST, JOURNALIST, AND POLITICIAN

To effectively reduce your level of pessimism or resignation, you must first admit and acknowledge that these behaviors are not productive and identify how and why they are having a negative impact on your work and personal life. One way to begin doing this is to observe the reactions that co-workers, family members, and friends have to your pessimistic or resigned behavior. What kind of reaction do you get when you say something like, "It will never work," or "There's no point in trying to change this or that."

Another way to measure the effects your negativity has on the people around you is to take an honest look at your track record with work and the duration of your personal relationships. If you are fired from a job every few years, or if you don't keep new friends for more than a few months, it's a sign that you are probably doing something that others find unpleasant or offensive. Misery may love company, but company rarely loves misery. In other words, very few people will choose to work or hang out with people who are habitually negative. Most people will avoid a pessimist like the plague. The truth is that we all have our own woes, and spending time with people who dwell on the dark side of every scenario just isn't an appealing way to spend our time.

Whether you want to admit it or not, much pessimism and resignation is the outgrowth of unresolved anger. Ask yourself, "What am I so angry or upset about?" or "What experience or belief is fueling my negativity?" This can become a rather intense process, so if you really want to get to the bottom of it, you might consider enlisting the assistance of a coach or counselor to guide your process.

A powerful way to combat pessimism and resignation is to make it a personal mission to seek out positive people and experiences. As an experiment, devote one full week to filling your mind with uplifting, inspiring, and positive stories, events, and people. Watch comedies and choose movies with happy endings. Ask friends to lend you books and articles that gave them hope and helped them to look on the brighter side of life. Attend a speech given by a motivational speaker without scoffing at the ideas, or order tape programs. Nightengale-Conant is a great resource. The idea is to fill your mind with everything positive that you can take in. At the end of this week, ask a close friend or associate if he or she has noticed any difference in you. You can't expect to turn the tide overnight, but you can expect to see a little bit of difference in the positive direction with each step you take.

Procrastination

I went for years not finishing anything. Because, of course, when you finish something you can be judged. I had poems re-written so many times I suspect it was just a way of avoiding sending them out.

ERICA JONG
POET AND AUTHOR

In general, the tasks we put off are things we consider unpleasant, stressful, or just plain painful! No wonder we want to avoid them. What's important to consider when you find yourself in this spot is that you are probably exaggerating the downside and missing the potential positives.

Here's a helpful technique for overcoming procrastination:

- Write down a few words to describe one of the projects, tasks, or action steps that you have been putting off.
- Make a numerical list of all the reasons you don't want to take this step.
- List as many benefits to taking this step as you listed reasons for not wanting to take it.
- Look at the big picture. Keep looking for and listing benefits until you can see this project or action step with a balanced perspective.
- Just start the work, to get some momentum going.
- Complete this task, or delegate it to someone else, within the next three days.

Feeling Overwhelmed

> *Determine the thing can and shall be done,*
> *and then we shall find the way.*
>
> ABRAHAM LINCOLN
> U.S. PRESIDENT

One of the most effective ways to increase your sense of being overwhelmed is to beat yourself up for feeling that way! So, if that's what you're doing, stop it right now. It can't possibly help and will only use up valuable energy that you could be devoting to moving forward.

To reduce the feeling of being overwhelmed, first identify your overall goal for a project. What will the project or task look like when it's complete? Unless you know this and have a sense of the big picture, it will be impossible to identify the necessary steps and put them into logical order. Once you know where you are going, create a list of tasks that need to be completed to accomplish the job. Look at your list of tasks and determine which ones need to be completed before other ones can begin, which tasks can be handled simultaneously, and which tasks must be done at the very end.

Create a linear "to do" list, numbering each task in chronological order. If there are tasks that can or should be done in the same time frame, give them the same number. That could mean that you have three number fours, or two number sevens. Creating this plan will allow you to see the entire process from beginning to end, with all of the steps in between.

Now, review your list and next to each item, write either the word, "do," or the word "delegate." If you write "delegate," also write to whom you can give this task. It might be a professional, a company, a student, or even a volunteer, depending on the level of expertise and experience necessary.

The idea is to focus your time on only those tasks that no one but you can do.

One Barrier at a Time

It has been my philosophy of life that difficulties vanish when faced boldly.

ISAAC ASIMOV
SCIENCE WRITER AND SCIENCE FICTION AUTHOR

Think of breaking through barriers as a way of cleaning house. You can only be in one room at a time, and trying to clean every room at once is sure to result in greater chaos. Choose the barrier that seems to be impeding your initiative the most and focus on it until you begin to experience some concrete improvements. Only at that point should you begin to work on one of the others. If you find that you're really stuck on one of your barriers, take the initiative to reach out to a qualified expert for assistance. Use your *Personal Brilliance Notebook* to keep track of your progress and reward yourself for your accomplishments.

CHAPTER 18

Intensifying INITIATIVE

The great thing in this world is not so much where we stand as in what direction we are moving.

OLIVER WENDELL HOLMES, SR.
PHYSICIAN, AUTHOR, AND POET

FUELING your power of initiative may very well be the most important thing that you ever do. People who have an intense desire to make things happen, actually make things happen. They take both their strengths and their weaknesses and turn them into powerful action.

Intensifying initiative is easier to do than it might first appear. Since all people have a natural desire to improve their lives, linking that desire with various forms of motivation makes taking initiative an enjoyable and rewarding practice.

AWARENESS
CURIOSITY
FOCUS
INITIATIVE

While learning to intensify your sense of initiative, it's a good idea to start with projects that you truly care about. What's going on in your family, place of work, neighborhood, or community that needs to be improved? What's missing in one of these domains that you strongly feel should be present? By taking on a project or setting a goal that's close to home and dear to your heart, you will automatically have more drive and desire to make a difference. You will also have easy access to resources and people who can join the effort you are launching. Don't try to change the world overnight. Start with something small, but meaningful. The next time you catch yourself saying, "Somebody should do something about that," take the initiative to be that person.

Initiatives in Action

Initiative #1

When Melba's two daughters were in elementary school, they walked a mile to a bus stop that was located at a gas station next to a very busy highway. The thought of her children and their friends waiting for a bus in such a high-traffic area worried her daily. Since there were more than a dozen children at this stop, the owner of the gas station had a policy that only two children were permitted inside the station at a time. On cold and rainy days, the children would stand huddled together or run back and forth along the highway in an attempt to stay warm until the bus arrived. Melba decided it was time to take action. First she wrote a letter to the school board expressing her concern. Weeks passed and although she made several calls to the school board office, she received no response except, "We're looking into it."

Not satisfied that they were really doing as they said, she went to the next school board meeting and expressed her concern so that her statement would be part of the public record. She was politely informed that the school district had more than 100 bus stops and they were doing their best to ensure that all of them were in safe locations. She pointed out that if the bus traveled just one half-mile further, the children could be picked up at the neighborhood playground, which was a safe distance from the highway and had a pavilion that the children could stand under in bad weather.

Another two months went by and nothing happened. Undaunted, Melba created a petition and circulated it among the parents of the children who were picked up at the gas station bus stop. Everyone was willing to sign. She sent the petition to the school board, and then called all the parents, asking them to attend the upcoming board meeting and to bring their children. This was the move that got the school board and the media's attention. Within two weeks of the meeting, the bus stop was officially relocated to the playground.

The key to being a successful initiator is to take responsibility for a change that needs to be made or a project that you feel is important. If everyone waits for someone else to take responsibility, nothing ever gets done. Regardless of how young, old, rich, or poor we might be, we all have the power to make a meaningful difference.

Initiative #2

One of the stories that touched thousands of people's hearts after 9/11 was the young boy who started a campaign to send gloves for the people digging through the rubble. He suggested that everyone buy one pair of gloves, sign them, and send them to a central location where they could be distributed to the workers and volunteers. The response he received was tremendous, and the hands and hearts of the people involved in the rescue and clean-up effort were warmed by his initiative. If an elementary school student can launch an initiative that makes a difference for thousands of people, imagine what you can do! Keep in mind that this young man started out with nothing but an idea (Awareness, Curiosity, Focus) and a deep desire to help others (Initiative).

Initiative #3

There is no doubt that there is strength in numbers. Taking an idea to an organization that will share your concern and enthusiasm is a great way to add power and momentum to your plan. For nearly seventy years, individual Lions Clubs and districts in the United States, Canada, and several other countries have collected used eyeglasses for distribution to the needy in developing nations. The Lions Club adopted the mission of making sight conservation their major goal after members heard an impassioned speech presented by Helen Keller at Cedar Point, Ohio, in 1925. In that speech, Helen challenged the Lions to become "Knights of the Blind," a challenge that has become a rallying cry for Lions' projects around the world. When one person enrolls a group of others in a worthy cause, there's no telling what can happen.

Initiative #4

In 1992, when McDonnell Douglas (which later merged with Boeing) was going through a series of unsettling layoffs, a young employee by the name of James Carter Williams came up with the idea for the Chairman's Innovation Initiative. Williams was quoted as saying: "There were strong people that were walking out the door. It seemed that rather than teaching them how to write resumes, we ought to figure how to leverage their skills." Beginning with that idea, Williams founded a group within the company to champion original and potentially profitable business ideas.

The idea really took off when Williams was asked to help solve two major concerns. The first was creating added value for shareholders. The second was providing an innovative outlet for company employees. The Chairman's Innovation Initiative is now a twenty-member business unit. In the past few years, it has reviewed more than 700 business plans. Williams's role is to work with employees to refine their plans and obtain financing from sources outside of Boeing.

One of the businesses that the Chairman's Innovation Initiative has launched is AVCHEM, a company that began by taking on the responsibility of managing hazardous materials for Boeing. AVCHEM now tracks hazardous materials like brake fluid, oil, paint, and solvents for a number of other companies.

Jumpstart Your Initiative

Sometimes all it takes to get going is a little jumpstart. The following methods and strategies can become habits with practice and persistence.

- Give yourself permission to decide for yourself
- Make choices and act on them.
- Don't wait to be inspired—get inspired.
- Increase your accountability.
- Live by your word.

Give Yourself Permission to Decide for Yourself

Few are those who see with their own eyes and feel with their own hearts.

ALBERT EINSTEIN
PHYSICIST

If you know that you have a good idea or a plan that will work, give yourself permission to move forward with the plan. Waiting for others to join you in your initiative can slow the wheels of innovation and drag out the process. As you build momentum, others will naturally want to jump on board.

One of the enemies of initiative is your attempting to gain consensus for all of your decisions. Obviously there are times when consensus is required, but when you have the knowledge and power to make a decision on your own, do it. While this may sound obvious to those of you who are already in the practice of making decisions, it's shocking how many people poll their circle of friends before they make such momentous decisions as, "Should I change my hairstyle?"

An important aspect to giving yourself permission to make your own decisions is learning to trust yourself. Particularly when it comes to personal decisions, the likelihood of someone other than you knowing what's best for you is very small.

Make Choices and Act on Them

The refusal to choose is a form of choice;
disbelief is a form of belief.

FRANK BARRON
CREATORS ON CREATING: AWAKENING AND
CULTIVATING THE IMAGINATIVE MIND

The longer it takes to make a decision or a choice, the longer you stay in status quo or stalemate. Keep in mind that you don't have to come up with the best possible decision, you just have to come up with one way that will work. The sooner you make a decision, the sooner you can take action.

Years ago I had the pleasure of hearing a speech given by Gracie Hopper, the first female rear admiral of the U.S. Navy. In that speech, she said, "It's often easier and faster to ask for forgiveness than to get permission." She wasn't suggesting that we recklessly break the rules and do our own thing without concern for the consequences. She was stressing that if you know that something is needed and you know you can take care of that need, do it! If it succeeds, your superiors will thank you. If it happens to fail, then make amends and try something new next time.

Admiral Hopper forbade anyone in her command to say, "Because that's how we've always done it," or "We tried that once and it didn't work." She empowered the men and women in her unit to trust their training, their judgment, and most of all, themselves.

Don't Wait to Be Inspired—Get Inspired!

Every man who knows how to read has it in his power to magnify himself, to multiply the ways which he exists, to make his life full, significant and interesting.

ALDOUS HUXLEY
ENGLISH NOVELIST

Here are some suggestions for intensifying your initiative:

- Commit to investing at least three hours each week to increasing your inspiration.
- Take advantage of every available resource to get yourself fired up for a project or venture that you want to pursue. Read a wide variety of articles, professional journals, trade magazines, and newspapers, all the while keeping your goals in mind. And don't limit your reading to your own area of expertise or the domain of your venture. Some of the best ideas are the result of looking to other types of businesses to find solutions for your own.
- Create a list of books, movies, motivational programs, and tapes that inspire you. Circulate the list to your friends or among your colleagues and ask them to add their favorites, so you can all benefit by each other's sources of inspiration.
- Read the biographies of people that you admire, and find out what they did and how they accomplished it. What

habits did they have that you can adopt? What problems did they face that are similar to your own challenges? How did they overcome obstacles? What did they do to inspire themselves?

- Attend motivational speeches, seminars, and workshops. Make it your goal to obtain at least one great idea that you can immediately implement or incorporate into your own life or business. One great idea often leads to many others.

Increase Your Accountability

Well done is better than well said.

BENJAMIN FRANKLIN
STATESMAN AND PHILOSOPHER

If you know that you're the one who is leading the charge, you don't sit around waiting for other people to accomplish what needs to be done. Unless someone is willing to be accountable, progress moves about as fast as molasses on a cold winter day.

Practice increasing your initiative by stepping up to the plate and volunteering to lead projects. Begin with projects that you have a good bit of expertise and experience in, but don't stop there. Once you've flexed your initiative muscles, stretch your comfort zone by taking on projects that require some additional training and education to bring you up to speed. By doing this, growth becomes a natural part of your everyday life. If we never take a risk, we stay where we are.

Sharing your goals with others is another way to increase your accountability. If, for example, you have a goal to exercise every day, team up with a partner or a group of people so that you can hold each other accountable. If you find that you are allowing outside influences to stop you from going to the gym after work, volunteer to be the designated driver to pick up one or more of the people in your exercise group. Many people who habitually change their own plans for a laundry list of reasons (excuses), will not drop the ball if others are counting on them.

Live By Your Word

Always do what you say you are going to do. It is the glue and fiber that binds successful relationships.

JEFFREY A. TIMMONS
THE ENTREPRENEURIAL MIND

People who accomplish what they set out to do keep their word to themselves and to others. Make a firm commitment to yourself that you will keep your promises, no matter what. The only permissible exception is your being truly too sick to get out of bed. Without living by such a strict standard, our lives can become a series of justifications and rationalizations. Whether we realize it at the time or not, every time we break a commitment, our belief in ourselves goes down a notch. To take initiative, we must believe in ourselves and be willing to follow through with our intentions.

You can have all the awareness, curiosity, and focus in the world, but without the catalyst of initiative, innovation simply won't happen.

PERSONAL BRILLIANCE IN EVERYDAY LIFE

CHAPTER 19

Making Brilliant, Everyday CHOICES

*An invasion of armies can be resisted, but
not an idea whose time has come.*

VICTOR HUGO
FRENCH NOVELIST, POET, AND DRAMATIST

IT TAKES ADULTS between twenty-one and twenty-eight
days of practice to break a habit or create a new one. That
means you're already well on your way to making awareness,
curiosity, focus, and initiative part of your daily life. Now that
you have harnessed the power of each of these catalysts, the
next step is to start putting them all together. The combined
power of these four strengths spins the wheel of your personal
brilliance and keeps it rolling.

One of the best ways to reinforce a habit is to keep it going
for at least 100 days. At that point it becomes second nature.
To give yourself the incentive to keep going, take a few minutes to assess the progress that you have already made. Go
back to the Web site as you did in Chapter 2, and repeat the
Personal Brilliance Quotient Assessment. The Web address is
www.MyPersonalBrilliance.com.

After completing the program in this book, many readers
have scored higher in three or all four of the catalysts, while
others have improved significantly in just one or two areas.

Once you've compared your new results with the old,
you'll know where you've improved. You'll also know to

which components you need to devote more practice, so you can bring your habits of personal brilliance into greater balance. For members of the Personal Brilliance community, exercises from our ever increasing catalog will be provided each time you visit the Web site.

Awareness, Curiosity, Focus, and Initiative in Action

The greatest discovery of my generation is that human beings can alter their lives by altering their attitudes of mind.

WILLIAM JAMES
PSYCHOLOGIST AND PHILOSOPHER

After a thirty-year banking career, John Huston used his awareness, coupled with his vast experience, to identify the positive economic impact that entrepreneurial businesses have in the creation of jobs in a community. Also applying curiosity, focus, and a great deal of initiative, John has played a huge part in galvanizing the angel investor community in Ohio to support entrepreneurial ventures in the area. He has created angel investor events in which entrepreneurs can make their innovations known and, as a result, is the cofounder of the only angel fund in Columbus, Ohio. Recognizing John's influence in the entrepreneurial community, Governor Bob Taft appointed John to the Ohio Venture Capital Authority. John's approach to this endeavor is a perfect example of personal brilliance at work. He used his experience, as well as his habit of personal brilliance, to create a new career that is tremendously helpful to his community.

Consider the late Charles Schulz. The *Peanuts* comic strip resonates with a broad audience, thanks largely to Schulz's awareness of everything from applied psychology to the way adults sound to children. After his death, Billie Jean King described Schulz's curiosity—how he called her to ask questions about competition and other issues. "He would probe and probe and probe, ask questions all the time." Extreme focus is apparent in the unforgettable characters and stories he created. And he had the initiative to persevere when an editor decided to stop publishing his comic strip five decades ago—and to continue touching lives long after he could have retired. His daughter said it was no coincidence that he died just as his final strip was being published.

With the habit of personal brilliance, you too will use your unique abilities to make a difference. Awareness and curiosity will illuminate your life, focus will intentionally direct those tremendous light beams, and initiative will push you to do something with all this ingenuity.

The Sky Is Not the Limit!

Even noble work is at first impossible.

THOMAS CARLYLE
SCOTTISH PHILOSOPHER AND AUTHOR

If you've read this entire book, congratulations! Understand that the development of your personal brilliance is an ongoing process, a journey. By reading this book and trying the exercises you have embarked on that journey. I hope you come back to this book and your *Personal Brilliance Notebook* regularly as you continue on this path.

Development takes time and significant effort. Your biggest challenge will be what you do with the information in this book now that you have completed it. How will you apply what you've learned? All of the strategies between these covers do work, but only if you use them.

We want to hear from you about your progress and your challenges. We have designed a Web site as a resource for you on your journey as you go to your next level: *www.MyPersonalBrilliance.com*. Please take advantage of the connection to share your progress with us.

The more innovative you become, the more your options in life increase and the more freedom you enjoy. There is tremendous power, comfort, and fulfillment in continuing to improve and expand your ability to innovate! Use your awareness in every situation, paying attention to everything. Be curious, asking questions from both wonder and doubt, focus on the two to three things you will try this week, and use your initiative to implement your newfound knowledge starting today.

One of the best ways to unlearn old habits and learn new ones is through repetition. It will be important for you to continue using and developing your natural gifts and practicing the daily habit of personal brilliance. As your mind adjusts to this new way of thinking and living, innovation will become a part of you. People will marvel at your abilities to respond to challenges, to come up with effective ideas and methods, and to solve difficult problems.

Best of all, you will begin to know that you have what it takes to face whatever comes your way. As your self-confidence increases, you will be willing to take more risks and go further out on a limb to get what you want. Not in a reckless way, but in a very planned, practiced, and powerful way. By experience, you will find out that you can succeed by your standards, on your terms. You will discover that you can live an extraordinary life of personal brilliance.

Index